Four Principles of Oppression:

160 Years of Eugenic Bigotry in U.S. Supreme Court Decisions, Supporting Involuntary Slavery, Sterilization and Commitment

1st Revision, October 2016

ISBN-10 1523884231
ISBN-13 9781523884230

Library of Congress Control Number: 2016903239

CreateSpace Independent Publishing Platform, North Charleston, SC

Note to Printer – pagination is intended to conform as closely as possible to the FRCP format for petitions to the Supreme Court of the United States, leaving the first four pages without numbers, as they can not form part of such a legal document

Note to Authors cited – You may have been quoted extensively, because your journalism and storytelling is far better than anything this author could hope to achieve. This work intends to bring all these stories together to advance the thesis that the Supreme Court of the United States has depended far too long upon fear and eugenic bigotry in its decisions; and to alert society to the terrible consequences of those decisions for millions upon millions of innocent and harmless citizens (including those millions denied life through the forcible sterilization of their potential forbearers, mostly poor and colored and disabled); and to encourage those with sufficient resources and fortitude to beard the Court in its own halls, with petitions to reconsider its many grievous errors. May this work serve to bring more attention to yours in this light. Without you, it would not have been possible.

For all those abused as children

who had the ability to play

removed by violence

Then when grown

refused

proud and productive work

for the sin

of not healing

Feared and treated

by their society

as dangerous

fit only to be abused

again

in the Courts

Review by A.J. Moore (Aug 2016):

http://www.midwestbookreview.com/rbw/aug_16.htm#moore

"There are many kinds of oppression. Dr. Baker's book is concerned with a particular form of oppression, one that has received relatively little attention in U. S. history. In his painstakingly researched book, Dr. Baker outlines how legislative authority and judicial process have been used to strip civil liberties from many thousands of people who have never committed a crime. ...

"As Dr. Baker makes his compelling case he reviews the history of relevant Supreme Court decisions. These, it turns out, reflect prevailing prejudices of the time rather than objective proof. ...

"If you choose to read this book, prepare for some very unusual and gripping reading."

Revised Forward (Oct 2016)

This book, citing a broad range of journalism, medical, legal, sociological and historical documents, and case law, traces an arc of bigotry in U.S. Supreme Court decisions, using similar language and reasoning, extending from slavery to eugenic sterilization to the death penalty to the treatment of prisoners to mental health. It demonstrates the High Court's often callous disregard for human life and liberty, in rendering prejudiced and flawed decisions with disastrous consequences to innocent and harmless people, which it then never bothers to review. It claims "stare decisis" for such decisions with pope-like infallibility.

For example, the 1927 Buck v. Bell eugenic sterilization decision, never overturned, forms the basis in both case law and procedure for modern mental health law and courts. In the case of the Virginia's Eugenical Sterilization Act, the Court accepted a defense attorney chosen from and by the prosecution, who apparently never called a witness or uttered an objection, the entire weight of "expert witnesses" on the side of the State, damning testimony by at least one "expert witness" who never examined Ms. Buck, and hearsay as proof. The Chief Justice, Oliver Wendell Holmes, justified the decision with the famous comment, "three generations of imbeciles is enough."

Hitler liked the Virginia Sterilization Act so much, he passed one just like it, almost verbatim, and used it to start the Holocaust. In the nearly 50 years following this decision, up into the

1970s, U.S. States sterilized over 60,000 U.S. citizens, mostly poor and colored, often without their knowledge or consent. As one white delivery doctor put it in about 1972, before sterilizing a Sri Lankan immigrant over her objections, "There are too many colored babies already."

The entire Buck v. Bell case may have fallen apart, if any Justice anywhere along the line had asked the simple question, "So, how well did she do in school?" Not only was Ms. Carrie Buck, whose illegitimate pregnancy followed rape by a member of her foster family, listed as a "good student", her daughter, the third of three alleged "generations of imbeciles", made the honor roll. Ms. Buck's sister was also sterilized without her knowledge or consent, merely for sharing the same blood.

The High Court never asked that question, never mind the impacts of its decision. In the 1942 Skinner v. Oklahoma case, repeated the "three generations of imbeciles" argument, without ever having asked or discovered the school grades of two of those generations. As a consequence of its later mental health decisions, sometimes based upon deeply flawed and prejudiced "expert witnesses", as in Barefoot v. Estelle, 1983, it granted psychiatric hospitals a legal indulgence to seduce and drag innocent and harmless people in, literally off the street, to drain their medical insurance with false involuntary commitments.

This book traces that language and reasoning all the way back to the 1856 Dred Scott slavery decision, which stated that "the negro might justly and lawfully be reduced to slavery for his benefit". In other words, for either his own good or the good of his master, as others have been sterilized or committed to mental hospitals.

So long as profiling remains acceptable for involuntary mental traumas and conditions, it will also be applied to gender and race. So long as this language and reasoning holds sway in the highest court in the land, so long as legal precedent and procedure can be based upon junk science, so long as civil liberties may be stripped from the harmless and innocent for the "good of society" ---

THEN BIGOTRY CAN NEVER DIE

— Don Baker, October 3, 2016

Forward (Feb 2016)

Given the Supreme Court's demonstrated power to maim futures and impose death, it is generations past time for it to show due diligence and humility, and to take responsibility for the consequences of its actions. Otherwise it is merely another stain upon the Constitution and its Amendments, and far more dangerous to our society than all the mass shooters combined.

This work is not legal advice, but an early draft petition to the Supreme Court of the United States (SCOTUS), requesting the Court to review, revise and reverse its decisions regarding eugenic sterilization, mental health and disability rights. It shows an arc of bigotry in Supreme Court language and reasoning stretching from at least Dred Scott (1856) to the present day, causing the massive loss of unborn life in millions, due to eugenic sterilizations from the 1920s to the late 1970s, and the untold suffering of millions more.

Written as close as possible to the Court-mandated form of such a petition, including pagination, this work is interspersed throughout with medical, legal, sociological and historical references, which might not match the form of a legal document. Sometimes courts have a tendency to close off a justly raised issue or avenue merely because of a poorly written petition. Therefore, the many reasons given in the "Reasons for Granting the Petition" section offer a variety of issues upon which more than one such petition could be based.

Be warned. Anyone following the Federal Rules of Civil Procedure (FRCP) can write a petition to the Supreme Court, but not everyone can succeed. The Court will consider perhaps only one in a hundred petitions, and Pro Se (without lawyer) petitioners tend to win only one in every hundred cases they file. Any error or disrespect can get a case thrown out. And non-lawyers outraged by sitting on the pointy end of biased Supreme Court decisions are more likely to make such errors than anyone. This I know by experience.

If you take this course, it is very likely that you are not a lawyer. For very few lawyers will gladly file discrimination cases for which they are not guaranteed profit and winning. Be prepared to lose time and again, for you will very likely make fatal mistakes. So if you are still determined to file - do an awful lot of research beforehand.

Note: The number of pages in this document far exceed the Rules. It contains multiple redundancies, and some non-collegial sharp opinions. It would have to be revised and rewritten to comply with the FRCP, and to constitute a compelling legal document.

– Good luck and good hunting, Don Baker, February 2016

(Cover Sheet)

No.____*(Assigned by Court Clerk)*____

In the
Supreme Court of the United States

Donald L. Baker, Ph.D. - Pro Se Petitioner
Otherwise your name

v.

The Supreme Court of the United States

A Direct Petition to the
Supreme Court of the United States
to Consider Reversal of Court Decisions
Regarding Eugenics and Mental Illness

Name and full contact information
goes here

TABLE OF CONTENTS

(Note: Table of Contents out of FRCP order here;
Forward and Afterward are not part of a legal document)

QUESTIONS PRESENTED

1. Whether this Court has used special, extralegal and discriminatory parens patriae criteria going back over 150 years through Buck v. Bell (1927) to Dred Scott (1856) to deprive civil liberties and equal status from certain unpopular classes of people, to wit:

Four Principles of Oppression

a- These people cannot be responsible for or control their actions, and are thus a danger to themselves and society;

b- Society has a right to defend itself against them by any legal procedure necessary;

c- Whatever society does to deprive them of civil rights and liberties is for their own good and benefit;

d- (Added in Buck v. Bell (1927), later enhanced, and never overturned) For their own benefit[1], these people may be deprived of civil rights, liberties and even body

---

[1] Buck v. Bell, 274 U.S. 200 (1927):

"that the sterilization may be effected in males by vasectomy and in females by salpingectomy, without serious pain or substantial danger to life; that the Commonwealth is supporting in various institutions many defective persons who, if now discharged, would become [Page 274 U. S. 206] a menace, but, if incapable of procreating, might be discharged with safety and become self-supporting **with benefit to themselves and to society** [emphasis added]" …

"that her welfare and that of society will be promoted by her sterilization" [emphasis added] …

"It is better for all the world if, instead of waiting to execute degenerate offspring for crime or to let them starve for their imbecility, society can prevent those who are manifestly unfit from continuing their kind." …

"Of course, so far as the operations enable those who otherwise must be kept confined to be returned to the world, and thus open the asylum to others, the equality aimed at will be more nearly reached."

parts on the basis of medical opinion, which shall not be considered punishment [2] [3] [4] [5] [6], and with which no lawyer or judge is competent to dispute or should interfere.

2. Whether these principles and resulting Decisions in and of themselves have caused massive, widespread and enduring prejudice, suffering and injustice far out of proportion to any alleged benefit to either society or the targets to which they have been applied, and far out of proportion to the standards of evidence, assumptions of guilt and dangerousness, and quality of justice required for criminal cases.

---

[2] O,Connor v. Donaldson, 422 U.S. 571 (1975): ""Now, the purpose of involuntary hospitalization is treatment and not mere custodial care or punishment if a patient is not a danger to himself or others. Without such treatment there is no justification from a constitutional stand-point for continued confinement unless you should also find that [Donaldson] was dangerous to either himself or others." 6 [422 U.S. 563, 571]"

[3] Addington v. Texas, 441 U.S. 418 (1979): "In a civil commitment, state power is not exercised in a punitive sense. [Footnote 4]: The State of Texas confines only for the purpose of providing care designed to treat the individual. As the Texas Supreme Court said in *State v. Turner,* 556 S W.2d 563, 566 (1977):

"The involuntary mental patient is entitled to treatment, to periodic and recurrent review of his mental condition, and to release at such time as he no longer presents a danger to himself or others.""

[4] Washington v. Harper, 494 U.S. 210 (1990): "The State might seek to compel Harper to submit to a mind altering drug treatment program as punishment for the crime he committed in 1976, as a "cure" for his mental illness, or as a mechanism to maintain order in the prison. The Court today recognizes Harper's liberty interest only as against the first justification."

[5] Foucha v. Louisiana, 504 U.S. 71 (1992): "Here, the State has no such punitive interest. As Foucha was not convicted, he may not be punished. Jones, supra, at 369."

[6] Kansas v. Hendricks, 521 U.S. 346 (1997): "The conditions surrounding confinement essentially the same as conditions for any civilly committed patient do not suggest a punitive purpose. Although the commitment scheme here involves an affirmative restraint, such restraint of the dangerously mentally ill has been historically regarded as a legitimate nonpunitive objective. Cf. *United States* v. *Salerno,* 481 U. S. 739, 747."

3. Whether through Buck v. Bell (1927, "three generations of imbeciles are enough"), modern mental health laws and courts share stare decisis with the Nazi Holocaust, and whether that and subsequent history establish that such Decisions have partaken of the fruit of the poisonous tree.

4. Whether the Court has allowed or enabled decisions regarding the mental health of criminals convicted of sometimes heinous crimes [7] [8] [9] [10] [11] [12] [13] [14] to be applied to

---

[7] Barefoot v. Estelle, 463 U.S. 880 (1983);

    stating that the psychiatric examination need not be done in person, but by prejudicial "hypothetical questions" (see Fitzsimons, GJ, & Shiv B, Nonconscious and Contaminative Effects of Hypothetical Questions on Subsequent Decision Making, Journal Of Consumer Research, Inc., Vol. 28, September 2001; *United States v. Parker*, No. 07-6239 (10th Cir., January 9, 2009); & Beecher-Monas, 2003), and that the outcome may be determined by "expert witnesses" whose methods of predicting future violence are less reliable (accurate one time in three; Monahan, 1981) than flipping a coin, and who may habitually be in the pay of one side for the purpose of producing desired results (see Tolson, Mike, 2004. Effect of "Dr. Death" and his testimony lingers; Doctor's effect on justice lingers/Testified in many death row cases; By Mike Tolson, June 17, 2004, Houston Chronicle)

[8] Fitzsimons, GJ, & Shiv B, Nonconscious and Contaminative Effects of Hypothetical Questions on Subsequent Decision Making, Journal Of Consumer Research, Inc., Vol. 28, September 2001,

    "even though such questions are purely hypothetical, respondents are unable to prevent a substantial biasing effect on their behavior. Further, we find that an increase in cognitive elaboration increases the contaminative effects of hypothetical questions and that this increase occurs primarily when the hypothetical information is relevant. In-depth poststudy interviews with a subset of the participants suggest that the effects of hypothetical questions on choice occur beyond awareness and, as a result, are quite difficult to counteract."

[9] Monahan, John, 1981, The Clinical Prediction of Violent Behavior, 1995 softcover ed., Jason Aronson, Inc., Northvale, NJ & London, 134 p., over 200 references

[10] *United States v. Parker*, No. 07-6239 (10th Cir., January 9, 2009); improper hypothetical questions during cross-examination of Parker's character witnesses

[11] Beecher-Monas, Erica, 2003, The Epistemology of Prediction: Future Dangerousness Testimony and Intellectual Due Process, Washington and Lee Law Review, Volume 60 | Issue 2, 3-1-2003,

"Two psychiatrists testified in *Barefoot* that the defendant "would probably commit further acts of violence and represent a continuing threat to society." They did not base their opinions on any personal examination of the defendant nor upon any history of past violent behavior-the defendant had prior convictions for drug offenses and unlawful possession of firearms, but had no history of violent crime. Instead, the experts based their testimony on a hypothetical question based on the crime and the defendant's conduct."

"Judges are the relevance gatekeepers for good reason. They have training in critical thinking, they are accountable to superior courts and to legal commentators, and they receive regular feedback regarding how well they have followed their procedures. They should not abdicate this important responsibility when it comes to expert testimony."

"A decision as important as a death sentence simply cannot be based on bunkum. No civilized country, much less one that prides itself on constitutional principles of due process, should tolerate expert witnesses confusing the jury with wholly unscientific assertions."

"Judges who evade the scientific issues presented by expert testimony perpetrate injustice. Providing the jury with misleading and unscientific evidence violates fundamental rule of law principles and due process and is intellectually indefensible. The consequences of misleading the jury in a death sentencing determination are severe, not only for the defendant, but also for a society that values justice and aspires to rationality."

[12] Tolson, Mike, 2004. Effect of "Dr. Death" and his testimony lingers; Doctor's effect on justice lingers/Testified in many death row cases; By Mike Tolson, June 17, 2004, Houston Chronicle),

citing that Dr. James Grigson, an expert psychiatric witness in Barefoot, was later reprimanded and expelled by the American Psychiatric Association for quackery and expelled by the Texas Society of Psychiatric Physicians for essentially becoming part of the prosecution team.

[13] Washington v. Harper, 494 U.S. 210 (1990),

affirming the State's interest in the involuntary administration of antipsychotic drugs, without a finding of incompetence, not necessarily for the benefit of a violent inmate, but as "an effective means of treating and controlling a mental illness likely to cause violent behavior"

"The hearing need not be conducted in accordance with the rules of evidence, and the state court's "clear, cogent, and convincing" standard of proof is neither required nor helpful when medical personnel are making the judgment required by the Policy."

"Nor is the Policy deficient in not allowing representation by counsel, since the provision of an independent lay advisor who understands the psychiatric issues is sufficient protection given the medical nature of the decision to be made." [Judges abdicating their duties to lay advisors]

people who have committed no crime, in order to control and subdue them to the

satisfaction of society, its prejudices [15] [16] [17] [18] [19] [20] [21] [22] [23] [24] [25] [26] [27] [28] [29] [30], and those who

---

[14] Kansas v. Hendricks, 521 U.S. 346 (1997)

"The Act's definition of "mental abnormality" satisfies "substantive" due process requirements. An individual's constitutionally protected liberty interest in avoiding physical restraint may be overridden even in the civil context. *Jacobson* v. *Massachusetts,* 197 U. S. 11, 26. This Court has consistently upheld involuntary commitment statutes that detain people who are unable to control their behavior and thereby pose a danger to the public health and safety, provided the confinement takes place pursuant to proper procedures and evidentiary standards. *Foucha* v. *Louisiana,* 504 U. S. 71,80. The Act unambiguously requires a pre commitment finding of dangerousness either to one's self or to others, and links that finding to a determination that the person suffers from a "mental abnormality" or "personality disorder." Generally, this Court has sustained a commitment statute if it couples proof of dangerousness with proof of some additional factor, such as a "mental illness" or "mental abnormality," see, *e. g., Heller* v. *Doe,* 509 U. S. 312, 314-315, for these additional requirements serve to limit confinement to those who suffer from a volitional impairment rendering them dangerous beyond their control. The Act sets forth comparable criteria with its pre-commitment requirement of "mental abnormality" or "personality disorder." Contrary to Hendricks' argument, this Court has never required States to adopt any particular nomenclature in drafting civil commitment statutes and leaves to the States the task of defining terms of a medical nature that have legal significance. Cf. *Jones* v. *United States,* 463 U. S. 354, 365, n. 13. The legislature is therefore not required to use the specific term "mental illness" and is free to adopt any similar term. Pp. 356-360."

[15] Skinner v. Oklahoma 316 U.S. 535 (1942)

"MR JUSTICE JACKSON concurring: … I also think the present plan to sterilize the individual in pursuit of a eugenic plan to eliminate from the race characteristics that are only vaguely identified and which, in our present state of knowledge, are uncertain as to transmissibility presents other constitutional questions of gravity. This Court has sustained such an experiment with respect to an imbecile, a person with definite and observable characteristics, where the condition had persisted through three generations and afforded grounds for the belief that it was transmissible, and would continue to manifest itself in generations to come. *Buck v. Bell,* 274 U. S. 200." **[Except that by their school records, Carrie Buck and her daughter were indeed _not_ imbeciles, but good students, which the Court apparently had not yet discovered 15 years after Buck, presumably because it had never requested any such records in order to make an informed judgment.]**

[16] Kindregan, Charles P., 1966, Sixty Years of Compulsory Eugenic Sterilization [CES]: Three Generations of Imbeciles and the Constitution of the United States, Chicago-Kent Law Rev., Vol 43(2):123-143, 1966

"At Nuremberg, American judges condemned the Nazi use of the German CES laws to eliminate "undesirable" characteristics from the race, but it was the American states which had "pioneered" the use of CES. The law is only as strong as the protection which it gives to its weakest subjects. Viewed by the standards of the Constitution of the United States, twenty-five states retain laws which are open to gross abuse of the rights of the most dependent and weakest citizens. ... Our science, our common sense, but most importantly our Constitution demand an end to CES in the United States." ...

"The decision in the *Davis* case was followed by another federal district court in *Mickle v. Henrichs 8* ", cites several conflicting decisions in Federal Courts as to whether sterilization was as "cruel and unusual" as castration, with some upholding sterilization on the basis that it had "no punitive intent", reasoning found in *** regarding involuntary mental "treatment".

[17] Mehler, Barry, 1987, 'Eliminating the Inferior: American and Nazi Sterilization Programs,' Science for the People (Nov-Dec 1987) pp. 14-18.

"Between 1928 and 1936, a number of European nations also passed sterilization laws, including Denmark (1929), Germany (1933), Sweden and Norway (1934), Finland and Danzig (1935), and Estonia (1936). All of these laws, according to Dr. Marie Kopp, who toured Germany studying the administration of Nazi Sterilization laws for the American Eugenics Society in 1935, were modeled and inspired by American efforts.(4)

"Furthermore, the American and German eugenicists were particularly close in ideology. Germans and Americans regularly translated each others literature, and the German movement was closely followed in the American eugenics press.

"In June of 1936, Heidelberg University planned a celebration in honor of its 550th anniversary. Harry Laughlin [who played a leading role as an absent "expert witness", who never saw Carrie Buck in Buck v. Bell, 1927], the author *of Eugenical Sterilization in the United States,* was offered an honorary degree in recognition of his services to eugenics.(5) Laughlin wrote that he would be glad to accept 'not only as a personal honor, but as evidence of the common understanding of German and American scientists of the nature of eugenics as research in and the practical application of those fundamental biological and social principles which determine racial endowments and the racial health... of future generations.'(6)"

[18] Pfeiffer, David, 1994, Eugenics and Disability Discrimination, Disability & Society, 9 (4), 1994, pages 481-99,

"People with disabilities, any disability, had their rights limited in the immediate past in the United States and still do so today by existing state statutes and the courts' incorrect interpretation of other statutes. They are constantly faced with the possibility of being deprived of fundamental rights that non-disabled persons enjoy. The great interest today in discovering which genes cause inherited impairments only accentuates the problem. As Rothstein (1992) points out, the Americans with Disabilities Act is only a first step toward fundamental changes necessary to avoid widespread discrimination based upon genetic testing. …

"Sterilization. During the nineteenth century and into the twentieth century sterilization was a common remedy for "feeblemindedness," as most disabilities were called. Before 1900 castration by removal of ovaries or testicles was the only method available for sterilization. During the third quarter of the nineteenth century the superintendent of the Winfield Kansas State Home for the Feebleminded castrated forty four boys and fourteen girls before being forced to stop for medical (not legal) reasons. However, around 1900 Dr. Harry Sharpe of the Indiana State Reformatory developed the procedure of vasectomy which is simple and cheap. About the same time in Europe the procedure of salpingectomy for women was developed. Sterilization on a large scale was then begun even though there was no legal basis for it. Dr. Sharpe alone sterilized six to seven hundred boys in the Indiana State Reformatory. (Burgdorf, 1980: 860)

"In Indiana in 1907 the first involuntary sterilization law in the country was enacted. By 1911 Washington, California, Connecticut, and New Jersey enacted involuntary sterilization laws. By 1930 a total of thirty three states had enacted such laws although in three states - New Jersey in 1913, New York in 1918, and Indiana in 1921 - the laws were struck down as unconstitutional. In Michigan a law was enacted, but struck down in 1918. Seven years later a version of the Michigan statute was accepted by the courts as constitutionally valid. The U.S. Supreme Court then upheld involuntary sterilization laws in 1927 in Buck v. Bell, 274 U.S. 200. …

"The U.S. Supreme Court in the Skinner Case found that the contention of inheritable criminal traits was sound. The law was struck down because it violated the principle of equal protection. …

"Another argument that Buck v. Bell is no longer the law of the land is the fact that in it the Court relied upon the police power of the state to uphold Virginia's compulsory sterilization law. The police power gives the state the right to act to protect the public health, safety, and welfare. While it is probably true that an argument based solely upon the police power would not be accepted by the Court, it is by no means certain. And in many cases the Supreme Court has agreed that the police power along with other powers of the state can be used to uphold a law or an action.

"Nevertheless, there are more persuasive arguments today for the legality of involuntary sterilization than the ones used by Holmes. In upholding the Virginia statute Holmes used the "rational basis" test. This test provides that if a rational basis for a statute can be established and that there are no other problems, the courts should not invalidate the act. The Court found a rational basis and therefore did not strike down the law. Scholars today (Murdock, 1974) contend that more than a rational basis would be needed to uphold a compulsory sterilization law for disabled people. While their argument may be correct, it is not relevant. The defense of involuntary sterilizations today is based upon the doctrine of parens patriae which means, in a loose way, "father power." That is, fathers - both biological and legal - know what is in the best interest of the "child" and can force the "child" to comply even if the "child" is an adult who happens to have a disability. …

"With some procedural modifications, the statute was upheld in NCARC v. North Carolina, 420 F.Supp. 451 (1976). In twenty two states a similar law exists … All that is necessary for sterilization of such a person is for the superintendent of an institution or a county director of social services to obtain a court order for it. In fact, it is the duty of the superintendent or county director to initiate such proceedings whenever the official feels it is in the person's best interest or the public's interest. If a superintendent or county director can convince a judge that a person with a disability can not manage day- to-day affairs, needs guidance, and would "benefit" from the sterilization, then the judge can order that it be done."
[Not very different from involuntary commitment]

[19] Nilsson, Kevin, circa 2000, Eugenics: A Historical Analysis,
http://campus.udayton.edu/~hume/Eugenics/eugenics.htm

"These proposals became law in April of 1924 when President Calvin Coolidge signed the Immigration Act. Interestingly, as Vice-President Coolidge had publicly stated that "America must be kept American. Biological laws show…that Nordics deteriorate when mixed with other races." (Kevles, 97) The act limited the number of European immigrants into the United States to a small percentage of the number of immigrants from the same country in 1890. … in 1890 few immigrants from the eugenically "inferior" regions of Eastern and Southern Europe immigrated to the United States. This clearly shows federal intent to block people of such European decent from supposedly tainting the Nordic races currently in the United States.

"The Nazi party took several steps to rid the Third Reich of the "causes of the disease." On July 14, 1933 the Cabinet passed the Law for the Prevention of Hereditary Diseases in Future Generations. This law, which was to be implemented on January 1, 1934 called for the sterilization of "lives unworthy of life". These "unworthy lives" included those persons suffering from congenital mental retardation, schizophrenia, manic-depressive insanity, epilepsy, Huntington's chorea, hereditary blindness, hereditary deafness, grave bodily malformation, and severe alcoholism. To enforce the sterilization laws, Nazi leadership created special "Hereditary Health Courts." All physicians were legally required to report to the courts anyone they encountered who fell into any of the categories for sterilization. As a result, by 1937 some 225,000 individuals had been sterilized by German authorities, a figure that was roughly ten times the number in the United States. (David, 91) Surprisingly, many eugenic supporters saw the rash tactics of Germany as a threat to the United States eugenic movement. Many began to argue that the United States was in fact sterilizing too few people. In 1934, Joseph S. DeJarnette, a key figure in Virginia eugenics said, "The Germans are beating us at our own game." (Kevles, 116)"

[20] Mostert, Mark P., 2002, Useless Eaters: Disability as Genocidal Marker in Nazi Germany, 2002, http://www.catholicculture.org/culture/library/view.cfm?id=7019&repos=1&subrepos=0&searchid=1 146140 © 2013 Trinity Communications

"However, relatively little attention has been paid to significant precipitating historical events that served as a catalyst for what later became known as the Holocaust. … Official notions of difference, which would later find their most diabolical expression in the murder of the Jews, were first expressed in state-sanctioned killings of children and adults with a wide range of physical, emotional, and intellectual disabilities."

"Societal tensions generated by deprivation, war, and notions of peoples' relative worth based on their ability to contribute to society continued to affect people with disabilities in institutions across Germany until the late 1920s, precipitating rapid and radical attitudinal changes even as the medical and psychiatric communities continued to struggle with custodial issues related to asylum inmates. It was clear, however, that extensive and expensive care could not be expended on people who could not immediately aid Germany's economic recovery. In practice, this meant that among asylum inmates, attempts were made to distinguish those who could be at least partially rehabilitated (the "curable") from those who could not (the "incurable"). By this time, two perceptions were firmly fixed among German medical professionals and laypeople alike. First, even the much lowered number of asylum inmates had to be further reduced in the long term, given the country's restricted economic outlook. Second, because many of those with disabilities were now more visible through outpatient programs, their infirmities and their sometimes inappropriate or undesirable behavior were often considered a threat to public decency and social order. Accordingly, inappropriate public behavior by people with disabilities was often dealt with in terms of legal action and through the criminal justice system, thus melding disability and criminality in the public mind. Professional and public debate had raised the imperative of social control to prevent the proliferation of asylum inmates, including those with disabilities, whose characteristic behaviors were now firmly perceived to be at best undesirable and at worst criminal."

[See also Addington v. Texas, 1979, regarding "protecting the community from the dangerous tendencies of some who are mentally ill" as evidence of this trend of thought; including "Due process does not require states to use the "beyond a reasonable doubt" standard of proof applicable in criminal prosecutions and delinquency proceedings. *In re Winship,* 397 U. S. 358, distinguished. The reasonable doubt standard is inappropriate in civil commitment proceedings because, given the uncertainties of psychiatric diagnosis, it may impose a burden the state cannot meet, and thereby erect an unreasonable barrier to needed medical treatment."]

[21] TENNESSEE V. LANE (02-1667) 541 U.S. 509 (2004), 315 F.3d 680,

"Justice Souter with whom Justice Ginsburg joins, concurring. ... the evidence to be considered would underscore the appropriateness of action under §5 to address the situation of disabled individuals before the courts, for that evidence would show that the judiciary itself has endorsed the basis for some of the very discrimination subject to congressional remedy under §5. Buck v. Bell, 274 U. S. 200 (1927), was not grudging in sustaining the constitutionality of the once-pervasive practice of involuntarily sterilizing those with mental disabilities. ... Laws compelling sterilization were often accompanied by others indiscriminately requiring institutionalization, and prohibiting certain individuals with disabilities from marrying, from voting, from attending public schools, and even from appearing in public. One administrative action along these lines was judicially sustained in part as a justified precaution against the very sight of a child with cerebral palsy, lest he "produc[e] a depressing and nauseating effect" upon others. State ex rel. Beattie v. Board of Ed. of Antigo, 169 Wis. 231, 232, 172 N. W. 153 (1919) (approving his exclusion from public school) ... Many of these laws were enacted to implement the quondam science of eugenics, which peaked in the 1920's, yet the statutes and their judicial vindications sat on the books long after eugenics lapsed into discredit."

[22] Grodin, Michael and George Annas, 2007, Physicians and torture: lessons from the Nazi doctors, Int'l Review of the Red Cross, Volume 89 Number 867 September 2007,

"The idea of racial hygiene emerged at the turn of the twentieth century, and the racial policies of the Third Reich were in many ways adapted from eugenics practices developed in the United States in the early twentieth century.12 Before the National Socialist Party came to power in Germany, there were already several institutes on racial hygiene at various German universities. The theories at these institutes grew out of the ''science of eugenics'' employed in the United States to justify government support for the twenty-three separate state laws which allowed for the involuntary sterilization of individuals.13 In the US Supreme Court decision Buck v. Bell, referring to the fact that the state can draft people into military service, the Court concluded,

"We have seen more than once that the public welfare may call upon the best citizens for their lives. It would be strange if it could not call upon those who already sap the strength of the State for these lesser sacrifices, often not felt to be such by those concerned, in order to prevent our being swamped with incompetence. It is better for all the world, if instead of waiting to execute degenerate offspring for crime, or to let them starve for their imbecility, society can prevent those who are manifestly unfit from continuing their kind. The principle that sustains compulsory vaccination is broad enough to cover cutting the Fallopian tubes. Three generations of imbeciles are enough.14

"Ultimately, the Nazis would carry this ideology beyond sterilization. They not only eliminated "undesirables" from their society, but also developed multiple programmes for the creation of a "master race", including the Lebensborn programme, which encouraged members of the SS to have children with women who had Aryan traits.15 **All the while they highlighted the "therapeutic" facet of their programmes, claiming that destroying the unworthy was "purely a healing treatment".16"**

"**They gave a medical connotation to their political movement, and often referred to Hitler as the "great doctor of the German people".18** [emphasis added]"

23 Stern, Alexandra Minna, 2005, "Sterilized in the name of public health: Race, Immigration, and Reproductive Control in Modern California", American Journal of Public Health | July 2005, Vol 95, No. 7, 1128-1138

"this statute had sanctioned over 20000 nonconsensual [and often uninformed] sterilizations on patients in state-run homes and hospitals, or one third of the more than 60000 such procedures in the United States in the 20th century."

"For the most part, *Madrigal v Quilligan* has been understood in light of the thousands of unwanted sterilizations reported in the United States from the late 1960s to the mid-1970s. And certainly, the experiences of the Mexican-origin women who suffered at the scalpels of County General physicians mirror those of the African American, Puerto Rican, and Native American women who came forth with comparable stories during the same years. Yet *Madrigal v Quilligan* should also be analyzed longitudinally, as a concluding link in the history of forced sterilization in modern California. Just as this case highlights the confluence of factors that facilitated sterilization abuse in the early 1970s, it also illuminates the longevity and potency of prosterilization arguments predicated on the protection of the public's health and resources."

24 Mariner, Wendy K., JD, LLM, MPH, George J. Annas JD, MPH, and Leonard H. Glantz JD, 2005, Jacobson v Massachusetts : It's Not Your Great-Great-Grandfather's Public Health Law, April 2005, Vol 95, No. 4 | American Journal of Public Health

"The Court did not require the state to demonstrate that sterilization was necessary and not arbitrary or oppressive. This suggests that the Court did not view *Jacobson* as having required any substantive standard of necessity or reasonableness that would prevent what today would be considered an indefensible assault. The Court did not even consider that Carrie Buck might have any right to personal liberty. With the Court's imprimatur of involuntary sterilization laws, more than 60000 Americans, mostly poor women, were sterilized by 1978.51" …

"The Court did not always say that danger meant an immediate threat to the public at large, and it accepted a broader range of means as reasonable. The Court generally accepted, with little analysis, the legislature's judgment of what should be done to protect public health and safety, at least where only individual liberty was affected. 52–54 In contrast, when state laws regulated commercial businesses and economic relationships, the Court typically required a close fit between goals and means.55 In *Lochner v New York*, which was decided 2 months after *Jacobson,* the Court struck down a New York state statute that limited the working hours of bakers to 60 hours per week, because it was "an unreasonable, unnecessary and arbitrary interference with the right and liberty of the individual to contract in relation to his labor." 56 The period between 1905 and 1937 is sometimes called the *Lochner* era, because the Court struck down many laws that regulated private economic relationships, such as labor laws, as a violation of property rights (also protected by the Due Process Clause) and freedom of contract.43" …

" By 1937, the Depression had shattered the belief that individuals could always take care of themselves, and the Roosevelt Administration pressed for reform legislation.58 An increasing number of justices and scholars recognized that economic survival and personal freedom required some affirmative government action to provide services and to regulate private industry. 59 … The Court began to routinely uphold state and federal legislation, and it accepted any plausible means a legislature chose to pursue legitimate ends, unless the law violated the Constitution.64–66" …

"Preserving the public's health in the 21st century requires preserving respect for personal liberty."

[see Plessy v. Ferguson, 163 U.S. 537 (1896), "Laws permitting, and even requiring, their separation in places where they are liable to be brought into contact do not necessarily imply the inferiority of either race to the other, and have been generally, if not universally, recognized as within the competency of the state legislatures in the exercise of their police power. The most common instance of this is connected with the establishment of separate schools for white and colored children, which has been held to be a valid exercise of the legislative power even by courts of States where the political rights of the colored race have been longest and most earnestly enforced. … Similar laws have been enacted by Congress under its general power of legislation over the District of Columbia, Rev.Stat.D.C. §§ 281, 282, 283, 310, 319, as well as by the legislatures of many of the States, and have been generally, if not uniformly, sustained by the courts." …

"So far, then, as a conflict with the Fourteenth Amendment is concerned, the case reduces itself to the question whether the statute of Louisiana is a reasonable regulation, and, with respect to this, there must necessarily be a large discretion on the part of the legislature. In determining the question of reasonableness, it is at liberty to act with reference to the established usages, customs, and traditions of the people, and with a view to the promotion of their comfort and the preservation of the public peace and good order. Gauged by this standard, we cannot say that a law which authorizes or even requires the separation of the two races in public conveyances [p551] is unreasonable, or more obnoxious to the Fourteenth Amendment than the acts of Congress requiring separate schools for colored children in the District of Columbia, the constitutionality of which does not seem to have been questioned, or the corresponding acts of state legislatures."

Ergo, for over 100 years, the Court has routinely deferred to legislatures (as follows), often despite any prejudice of the majority which limits the rights of minorities.]

[see In re Gault - 387 U.S. 1 (1967), "Legislatures are, as this Court has often acknowledged, the "main guardian" of the public interest, and, within their constitutional competence, their understanding of that interest must be accepted as "well nigh" conclusive. ... These factors, in combination, suggest that legislatures may properly expect only a cautious deference for their procedural judgments, but that, conversely, courts must exercise their special responsibility for procedural guarantees with care to permit ample scope for achieving the purposes of legislative programs."]

[see O'Connor v. Donaldson, 422 U.S. 563 (1975), "Rather than inquiring whether strict standards of proof or periodic redetermination of a patient's condition are required in civil confinement, the theory accepts the absence of such safeguards but insists that the State provide benefits which, in the view of a court, are adequate "compensation" for confinement. In light of the wide divergence of medical opinion regarding the diagnosis of and proper therapy for mental abnormalities, that prospect is especially troubling in this area and cannot be squared with the principle that "courts may not substitute for the judgments of legislators their own understanding of the public welfare, but must instead concern themselves with the validity under the Constitution of the methods which the legislature has selected." In re Gault, 387 U.S., at 71 (Harlan, J., concurring and dissenting)."]

[see Kansas v. Hendricks, 521 U.S. 346 (1997), Indeed, we have never required state legislatures to adopt any particular nomenclature in drafting civil commitment statutes. Rather, we have traditionally left to legislators the task of defining terms of a medical nature that have legal significance."]

[see Pennhurst State School v. Halderman, 465 U.S. 89 (1984), Dissent, "Throughout its history, this Court has derived strength from institutional self-discipline. Adherence to settled doctrine is presumptively the correct course. [Footnote 2/47] Departures are, of course, occasionally required by changes in the fabric of our society. [Footnote 2/48] When a court, rather than a legislature, initiates Page 465 U. S. 165 such a departure, it has a special obligation to explain and to justify the new course on which it has embarked."]

[25] McGuan, Elizabeth A. (2009) "New Standards for the Involuntary Commitment of the Mentally Ill: "Danger" Redefined," *Marquette Elder's Advisor: Vol. 11: Iss. 1, Article 10.* Available at: http://scholarship.law.marquette.edu/elders/vol11/iss1/10,

"**19.** Hortas, *supra* note **18,** at **159.** Thirty states enacted compulsory sterilization laws. *Id.* As recently as the 1920s, consistent with Hitler's extreme position of the eugenics movement, state legislatures in the United States were considering the idea of killing the mentally ill. *Id.* At **160.**"

"248. Scherer, *supra* note 4, at 364 n.11. "Permitting civil commitment on a strict medical model alone could erode rights of individuals due to medical error or inaccurate scientific theories." *Id.; see* CHEMERINSKY, *supra* note **70,** at 813-14 (discussing the eugenic sterilization of Carrie Buck, whom the Court described as "feeble minded," but who was later discovered to be of normal intelligence (citing Buck v. Bell, 274 U.S. 200, 205 (1927))). "

[26] Hortas, Laura E., *Asylum Protection for the Mentally Disabled: How the Evolution of Rights for the Mentally Ill in the United States Created a "Social Group,"* 20 CONN. J. INT'L L. 155, 159 (2004). In addition to the stigma of being mentally ill, the elderly mentally ill also face "ageism," which is defined as "prejudice towards, stereotyping, or discrimination against persons based solely on chronological age..." Williams, *supra* note 5, at 443.

[27] Scherer, Rachel A., *Toward a Twenty-First Century Civil Commitment Statute: A Legal, Medical, and Policy Analysis of Preventative Outpatient Treatment,* 4 IND. HEALTH L. REV. 361, 382-83 (2007) (explaining the reasons the mentally ill end up in the criminal justice system).

[28] Akin, John Warren, 2009, Inherited Realities: Eugenics, Oliver Wendell Holmes, Jr., and *Buck v. Bell,* *The Tower,* Vol 1, Number 2, Spring 2009

"It was the first cousin of Charles Darwin, Sir Francis Galton, who originally coined the term "eugenics" by deriving it from the Greek term meaning "well born" (Engs, 2005, p. 82). Contemporary doctrines from the fields of mental health and criminal psychology in the late 1800s dictated that problems of mental incompetence, criminal behavior, degeneracy, epilepsy, schizophrenia, and many other conditions were not only beyond treatment in many cases, but were almost always the direct result of heredity and lineage. As such, the belief arose that many individuals who were deemed "feeble minded" or otherwise mentally deficient needed to be prevented from procreating for the ultimate good of society."

"(*Buck v. Bell*, 1927). … The judgment of the Supreme Court was handed down in May of 1927, and the results rocked the foundations of the mental health system. The opinion was authored by Justice Oliver Wendell Holmes, Jr., a highly respected jurist and Civil War veteran. Only two pages in length, the opinion not only upheld the fundamental constitutionality of these programs, but forever framed into history his relentlessly analyzed belief that "three generations of imbeciles are enough" (*Buck v. Bell*, 1927). Based on an analysis of the procedural safeguards contained within the statute, Holmes and the majority held that the statute afforded adequate protection to satisfy the requirements of the 14th Amendment. Addressing the substantive legal question at hand, Holmes deferred to the elected legislature and ruled the practice constitutional."

"Selected for their particularly great need of procedural protections, African-Americans in the pre-Civil Rights era Deep South present ideal candidates for research. Often subject to abuse by segregated society, these citizens found themselves at the mercy of a legal process in which they had little control. Georgia has records of 4,933 patients being involuntarily sterilized, and after obtaining 1,649 cases, a sub-sample of all the African-American patients from Milledgeville's large integrated state hospital was chosen for study. They represent a time period spanning from 1939 through 1953, and provide a glimpse into the inner-workings of the South's eugenics programs."

"Of the several hundred files examined, only 52 contained any correspondence on behalf of the patient. The vast majority contained only the four requisite documents: an application to the Board by the Doctor or superintendent, the notice of the Board meeting sent to the guardian or next of kin, a report of the operation, and the original recommendation letter from the doctor or superintendent to the Board. Far too many of these patients simply lacked anyone on the outside who understood or cared for their plight. It must also be noted that national census data from 1940 indicates the illiteracy rate for blacks was over five times the rate for whites. The reality in the South was certainly even worse than that, and in the previous century 80% of black Americans were illiterate ("National Assessment of Adult Literacy", 2008).

"Of the 52 files containing correspondences, 33 were either dictated because of an individual's inability to read or write, written in confusing and incredibly poor child-like handwriting, or contained multiple serious grammatical errors that, at best, evidenced a grade school education. 26 exhibited a fundamental misunderstanding of the entire basis for the operation. All eugenic operations shared a common goal explicitly stated in the notices from the Board of Eugenics: the betterment of society's gene pool. These 26 letters, however, all consented to the procedure on the basis that these operations were in the best interests of the patients and not society, and that they would somehow help alleviate the medical conditions of the individual. These people simply did not understand what they were being notified of. One mother even begged in a barely legible note, "I don't want you to kill my son" (GA Case 1528), while another note was scratched out on the back of an index card with a return order from a retail store on the reverse (GA Case 1367). "Whatever you think is best for my..." is a sentiment commonly found throughout the letters, while anything even remotely relating to the betterment of society is conspicuously absent. In many cases, eugenic sterilization was a condition for patients' release back to their families.

"Particularly striking are the appeals. Of the 52 correspondence case files, 11 cases did not give consent. Yet of these 11, ten were sterilized anyway with no record of resolution in their files, only the objections of their family members and the dates they were ultimately sterilized. What unique characteristic allowed the one remaining patient to have their case dropped and forego sterilization? This inmate also has the distinction of being the only one who retained a lawyer, and was subsequently able to file a proper appeal in accordance with their strict guidelines. Only one other appeal, filed without the aid of legal counsel, is found in the record. This appeal was rejected without consideration because it was "filed incorrectly," and the patient was subsequently sterilized (GA Case 1636).

"Ultimately, the most conspicuous problem that arises in these case studies is that the law and the procedural safeguards it contains both presuppose a very high level of literacy and legal competence." **[In other words, this Court assumed theoretical procedural safeguards, to those they were supposed to protect, of Constitutional rights that it could never guarantee.]**

[29] Rubin, Nilmini Gunaratne, 2012, A crime against motherhood - Involuntary sterilization was a horrifying exercise in genetic engineering, Los Angeles Times, May 13, 2012,
http://articles.latimes.com/2012/may/13/opinion/la-oe-rubin-eugenics-mothers-day-20120513

"He didn't ask permission to perform the hysterectomy. In fact, he ignored her pleas. "There are too many colored babies already," he told her. Exhausted from labor, my mom was too weak to resist ... My mom was among the uncounted others who were coercively sterilized by overzealous private doctors acting on their own. Medical privacy laws make it hard to learn how many were victimized this way.

It was a horrifying exercise in genetic engineering. The intent was to strengthen the gene pool and reduce welfare rolls. The victims were usually women, including African Americans, Asians, Jews, Latinos, Native Americans, alcoholics, the disabled, epileptics, illiterates, the mentally ill, petty criminals, the poor, the promiscuous, rape victims and "anyone else who did not resemble the blond and blue-eyed Nordic ideal the eugenics movement glorified," as Edwin Black noted in his book "War Against the Weak."" **[So much for procedural safeguards – this Court cannot guarantee the souls of men.]**

[30] Wikipedia, 2013, Political abuse of psychiatry in the Soviet Union,
http://en.wikipedia.org/wiki/Political_abuse_of_psychiatry_in_...,

K. Fulford, A. Smirnov, and E. Snow state: "An important vulnerability factor, therefore, for the abuse of psychiatry, is the subjective nature of the observations on which psychiatric diagnosis currently depends."[185] According to American psychiatrist Thomas Szasz, these authors, who correctly emphasize the value-laden nature of psychiatric diagnoses and the subjective character of psychiatric classifications, fail to accept the role of psychiatric power.[186] Musicologists, drama critics, art historians, and many other scholars also create their own subjective classifications; however, lacking state-legitimated power over persons, their classifications do not lead to anyone's being deprived of property, liberty, or life.[186] For instance, plastic surgeon's classification of beauty is subjective, but the plastic surgeon cannot treat his or her patient without the patient's consent, therefore, there *cannot* be any political abuse of plastic surgery.[186] The bedrock of political medicine is coercion masquerading as medical treatment.[187]:497 What transforms coercion into therapy are physicians *diagnosing* the person's condition a "illness," *declaring* the intervention they impose on the victim a "treatment," and legislators and judges *legitimating* these categorizations as "illnesses" and "treatments."

[187]:497 In the same way, physician-eugenicists advocated killing certain disabled or ill persons as a form of treatment for both society and patient long before the Nazis came to power.[187]:497 Szasz argued that the spectacle of the Western psychiatrists loudly condemning Soviet colleagues for their abuse of professional standards was largely an exercise in hypocrisy.[186][145]:220 According to Szasz, the problem, from which psychiatric abuse stems, is psychiatric power that is just as prevalent in democratic societies as it was in the USSR.[186][145]:220 He stated that psychiatric abuse, such as people usually associated with practices in the former USSR, was connected not with the misuse of psychiatric diagnoses, but with the political power built-in to the social role of the psychiatrist in democratic and totalitarian societies alike.[186][145]:220 In a 1994 article Szasz stated that "the classification by slave owners and slave traders of certain individuals as Negroes was scientific, in the sense that whites were rarely classified as blacks. But that did not prevent the 'abuse' of such racial classification, because (what we call) its abuse was, in fact, its use."[186] The collaboration between psychiatry and government leads to what Szasz calls the "therapeutic state", a system in which disapproved actions, thoughts, and emotions are repressed ("cured") through pseudomedical interventions.[188]:17 Thus suicide, unconventional religious beliefs, racial bigotry, unhappiness, anxiety, shyness, sexual promiscuity, shoplifting, gambling, overeating, smoking, and illegal drug use are all considered symptoms or illnesses that need to be cured.[188]:17 According to Szasz, "the therapeutic state swallows up everything human on the seemingly rational ground that nothing falls outside the province of health and medicine, just as the theological state had swallowed up everything human on the perfectly rational ground that nothing falls outside the province of God and religion."[187]:515

would benefit financially from their civil commitment [31] [32] [33] [34], in manners and methods which would shock the conscience in any other field of law or medicine [35] [36] [37] [38] [39] [40] [41].

---

[31] Kerr, Peter, 1992, Government review finds 64% of psychiatric hospital stays aren't needed, New York Times News Service April 29, 1992,

"A federal government review of private psychiatric hospital cases -- most of them teen-agers and young children of military families -- has found that in 64 percent of the cases, patients never should have been admitted or were kept longer than necessary or their hospitals could not justify treatment with their medical records. The abuses may have cost U.S. taxpayers hundreds of millions of dollars."

[32] Boodman, Sandra, 1992, Ads for Psychiatric Hosptials Come Under Attack, The Washington Post, May 08, 1992,

"Many of these ads--the centerpieces of aggressive, multimillion-dollar marketing campaigns— suggest that rebellious, moody and even unconventionally dressed adolescents, disobedient children and those with poor grades might be seriously mentally ill."

"Between 1980 and 1986 [coincident with Barefoot, 1983], admissions of juveniles to private psychiatric hospitals nearly tripled, rising expansion of inpatient psychiatric care for children and adolescents was fueled by parental insecurities, the elasticity of psychiatric diagnoses, the willingness of insurance companies to pay for hospitalization and relentless marketing by the hospitals themselves."

[33] Sileo, Chi Chi, 1994, Rip-off depress mental health care – fraud in psychiatric hospital practices, Insight on the News, Jan 24, 1994,

"Robbins's story may be bizarre, but it has an age-old explanation: greed. "I asked one doctor, |Why are you people doing this?'" she says. "And he looked me in the eye and said, This is how we get money from the insurance companies.'" Her insurance company forked over $8,397 for her treatment."

[34] Nadler, Art, 1998, Several claim they've been hospitalized against their will, Las Vegas Sun, Jan 24, 1998,

"Under a state law called a Legal 97, anyone in Nevada exhibiting signs of mental illness can be picked up and held against his will in a mental institution. All it takes is for a spouse, parent, adult child, legal guardian, physician, psychologist, social worker or registered nurse to say you are mentally ill. The argument is usually that you are posing a threat to yourself or others around you. Once one of these people puts a Legal 97 in motion, and you're involuntarily transported to a mental facility, your freedom is lost for 72 hours. Of course you can call someone -- friends, the police, your congressman -- but if you say you're calling from a mental institution, your credibility takes a serious nosedive.

"Las Vegas attorney Hamilton Moore is representing 15 people in Nevada who have filed a class action lawsuit who claim they were involuntarily committed and held in private mental hospitals. He said he has talked to more than 100 people since 1989 who said they had similar experiences. One case cited by Moore involves a man who was involuntarily committed last fall to Charter Behavioral Health System of Nevada after he was brought to University Medical Center. A Charter nurse recommended that the man be admitted, citing, among other things, that the man threatened his sister, Moore said. But his sister denies that her brother threatened her."

"Laurie Palatt went to the Valley Hospital emergency room on Nov. 4, 1996, with severe stomach pains. When she arrived, she said, a nurse did an ultrasound test and said she was pregnant. When Palatt, 48, told the emergency room doctor that she was pregnant, she said her sister who accompanied her told th physician that she was imagining it and that she had given a car away recently. She said the ER doctor called Charter Hospital, and they dispatched a nurse. Palatt said she was strapped to a table with leather restraints on her wrists and ankles. After Palatt spent several hours in this position, a Charter Hospital nurse arrived. Palatt said that after some questioning, and taking into account what Palatt's sister had said, the nurse determined that she was hearing voices and ruled that she should be held for 72 hours. Palatt wasn't taken to Charter Hospital. She believes that was because she didn't have health insurance. Instead, she was transported to the state Southern Nevada Adult Mental Health Services facility, 6161 W. Charleston Blvd. At Adult Mental Health, a psychiatrist examined Palatt and determined that there was "no evidence of psychosis" and that she was "in good behavioral control." She was released, ending a 21-hour ordeal. "I lost my husband (in a divorce shortly after this incident), my home, my baby and my job," Palatt said. "I worked in child care, and I can't work with children with this on my record.""

[35] Electric Shocks Are Inhumane And Barbaric, http://www.cchrflorida.org/blog/electric-shocks-areinhumane-and-barbaric/ and http://www.youtube.com/watch?v=RIJ10qnrfl4&

A developmentally disabled young boy of color, at a mental facility named after a Judge, restrained and given many successive electric shocks for refusing to remove a jacket, in the name of a "treatment modality" following the behavior modification methods of Skinner.

[36] Baker, DL, Oct 2014, Origins and Effects of SCOTUS Mental Health Rulings: A Reading List, independent.academia.edu/DonaldLBaker/,

applying the reasoning in Barefoot (1983) to another medical field: "Don't worry about a thing – although your heart surgeon has never seen either you or your medical record, he has heard about you through hypothetical questions and there is no convincing evidence that he is almost entirely unreliable."

[37] Mohr, Wanda K., 1998, Experiences of patients hospitalized during the Texas mental health scandal, Perspectives in Psychiatric Care, Vol 34, 1998,

"FINDINGS. subjects (N = 19) voiced complaints about the stigma resulting from the hospitalization as well as lack of individual care, violations of personal boundaries, ineffectual outcomes, permanent disruption to family relations, separation from family, trauma of seeing others restrained, and being restrained themselves."

[38] Sileo, 1994:

"When Karen Robbins saw the advertisement for a new weight-loss center, she thought it was just what she needed. She called the 800 number and was told that, if she signed up, she would be treated in a beautiful residential spa in Florida, complete with hiking trails, a swimming pool, a structured diet and daily counseling. Best of all, her insurance would cover the whole cost -- even her first-class airfare to Florida. The Harbor Springs, Mich., woman spent the next three months preparing herself and her family for her departure, and dreamed of a slimmer, happier future.

"But those dreams came to a screeching halt with her first look at the spa. "One hour after I got there," she says, "I wanted out."

"The hiking trails, swimming pool and counselors were nowhere to be seen; instead, Robbins found herself in a cheerless, chaotic hospital peopled with a rude staff an screaming obscenities. Robbins says she was placed in a tiny, filthy room; stripped of all her personal belongings; and told promptly that she was severely bulimic and suicidally depressed. She was also told, she says, that the hospital could keep her for 72 hours under involuntary commitment laws because she was a danger to herself and others.

"I may be fat," Robbins says, "but I'm not crazy." Rejecting the diagnosis, Robbins called her husband, Al, and asked him to come to get her. But a day later she signed an order to rescind her release -- under pressure, she says, from the center's staff. "They wouldn't allow me to go to the cafeteria and get food," she says, "unless I signed" She was kept, she says, under medication and "in complete terror" for a week before she was finally able to leave. When her husband came for her, she was in such bad shape he almost didn't recognize her."

"Schwartz's research has found that up to 75 percent of children in psychiatric institutes (currently around 300,000, a number that represents a 400 percent increase in the past decade) are unnecessarily hospitalized. "Parents are just dumping their children," says Stout of Forest Hospital. And some hospitals kept them in the dark, so that even if the parents were truly well-meaning, they had no idea what was really happening to their kids."

"You couldn't get away with treating criminals this way," says Schwartz, who notes that many of these children are under the age of 13. "This whole thing is frightening on many levels. It's a violation of civil rights. It's the medicalization of deviant behavior. And it's racist and elitist. Most of these kids are white and upper middle class; amazingly, there are almost no black or Native American children who are |acting out' or |aggressive' -- just black or Native American children who are assaultive and delinquent. And these children are being tagged with a label and a stigma that will haunt them the rest of their lives."

"That last fear is not misplaced. A stay in a psychiatric hospital, even as a child, remains on a person's medical record. And a study by the National Institute of Mental Health in 1993 found that even ex-convicts rank above former mental patients in societal acceptance. "The stigma is incredible," says a patient. "You can't tell anyone except your most trusted friends. Forget telling an employer! Sometimes they find out anyway, and all of a sudden you're unfit to work there."

"The abuse by some psychiatric hospitals is harming two kinds of hospital patients, experts say: those hospitalized unnecessarily and against their will and those who need hospitalization but aren't getting it because of their mistrust of the services or because some hospitals and insurance companies are cutting back on the services they'll provide or fund. And of course, everyone suffers when insurance companies get ripped off -- to the tune of higher premiums for all."

[39] Smith, Mark, 1992, PROFITABLE ADDICTIONS/Abuses in mental health programs are pinpointed, WED 04/29/1992 HOUSTON CHRONICLE, Section A, Page 1, 2 STAR Edition

"The GAO report, released Tuesday during a congressional hearing on abuses in the private psychiatric hospital industry, also found nearly two-thirds of the mental health claims filed to the Civilian Health and Medical Plan for the Uniformed Services, or CHAMPUS, were for treatment considered medically questionable. The report -- presented to the House Select Committee on Children, Youth and Families -- is the result of growing concern in Congress and the Department of Defense about the number of CHAMPUS mental health claims, which more than doubled between fiscal years 1985 and 1989. Texas led the nation with the greatest number of these claims, $132 million in fiscal 1990 or about a fifth of all claims. Texas became the focus of a state and federal probe last year after a 14-year-old San Antonio youth, covered by CHAMPUS, was picked up by a private security firm and taken to a private psychiatric hospital. His admission to the facility was based on the diagnosis of a doctor the youth never saw. It took a court order to gain his release. In CHAMPUS claims, California was a distant second with $95 million in fiscal 1990, followed by Florida with $65 million and Virginia and Georgia with $34 million each. U.S. Rep. Patricia Schroeder, D-Colo., the panel's chairwoman, said reports of private psychiatric hospital abuse have been "one of the most disgraceful and scandalous episodes in the history of health care in America.""

"The panel also learned that federal agents are investigating the use of patient "bounty hunters" by private psychiatric hospitals at overseas U.S. military bases. Investigators said they received reports that private psychiatric hospitals pay "bounties" or kickbacks to Defense Department employees for the transport and delivery of military employees and their dependents. With growing reports of patient "headhunters" and bounties, U.S. Rep. John Bryant, D-Dallas, introduced federal legislation Tuesday that would outlaw the practice nationwide. Texas lawmakers last fall passed a similar law. But most states, Bryant said, lack such legislation." [A direct result of the powers granted to "medical opinion" in civil commitment issues by this Court in Buck, 1927, to present day]

[40] Smith, Mark, 1991, PROFITABLE ADDICTIONS/Captured and held against will/Some private hospitals prey on patients with insurance, MON 09/09/1991 HOUSTON CHRONICLE, Section A, Page 1, 2 STAR Edition

"For Marianne Harrell, April 12 was a flashback to her childhood in Nazi Germany. Two huge men came to take her 14-year-old grandson away. They were private security company employees, and their mission was to deliver the youth to a corporate psychiatric hospital. The teen-ager had not been physically evaluated by a doctor. Instead, the decision to come for him was made based on comments from his 12-year-old brother to a psychiatrist."

"For Harrell, 56, the incident continues to haunt her despite the seeming safety of her San Antonio suburb. She now never leaves her doors unlocked - even when she is home. She cringes whenever she sees a patrol car. The men were from Sector One, a now-defunct San Antonio-based security company. They told Harrell and her husband, Sid, that they were to pick up the youth and deliver him to a private psychiatric hospital. "They told us: `If he doesn't go for 24 hours we'll get a warrant and he'll stay 28 days and he'll have a record,'" Harrell said, fighting back tears. "They act just like the Gestapo when people used to walk in people's homes and take them out in the street." After they picked up the teen-ager, one of the security officers applied for and received an emergency apprehension and detention order. The order was based on the apparent medical diagnosis of Dr. Mark Bowlan, a Colonial Hills Hospital assistant medical director who never examined or treated the teen-ager before he was picked up. [A direct result and responsibility of this Court (Barefoot, 1983) endorsing the use of diagnosis by hypothetical questions without directly examining the patient being diagnosed.] … Bowlan has since resigned and his medical license was revoked after he was found to have submitted forged documents to the State Board of Medical Examiners to gain a medical license."

"Beverly Williams, 51, ... said she was dragged out of her bathroom by two security guards and handcuffed on an emergency apprehension and detention warrant. ... Sector One employees came for Beverly Williams early in the evening of March 19, acting on a diagnosis made by a doctor who had not evaluated her in person. Beverly Williams said she had just learned her ex-husband had remarried and had been drinking and her daughter called the doctor to express concern. "I went into the shower and I was getting my water ready and I heard the dog bark," she said. "I opened up the bathroom door to look out and I said: `What are you doing to my dog?' There was a Mexican man and a black man and they grabbed me. "I said to them: `I'll go with you.' I begged them to let me put some clothes on. They carted me out in front of my neighbors. My bathrobe was just on my shoulders and it kept falling off." Upon arriving at Colonial Hills Hospital, she said, the medical staff would not let her make any phone calls, nor was she read patient rights. She claims she was intimidated into signing voluntary commitment papers. Beverly Williams, considered "a model employee" by her employer, said she was so embarrassed and humiliated by the experience that she has tinted the windows of her car so neighbors can't see her when she leaves her home."

[41] Smith, Mark, & Cindy Rugeley, 1993, State probes psychiatric care of youth Morales checks into legality of expensive hospitalizations, SUN 11/21/1993 HOUSTON CHRONICLE, Section A, Page 1, 2 STAR Edition

"Hundreds of Texas children were placed, perhaps unnecessarily, in costly private psychiatric hospitals at a taxpayer expense of about $800 a day because of lenient state and federal Medicaid rules and a lack of outpatient alternatives. Texas Attorney General Dan Morales is studying whether the hospital admissions, which totalled almost $70 million during the last budget year, may have violated new state laws or previous court agreements with psychiatric hospital chains. … The program -- known as the Early and Periodic Screening, Diagnosis and Treatment Comprehensive Care Program – originally was designed to pay for the early detection and treatment of medical and dental problems for poor children under the state Medicaid program."

"Payments to private psychiatric hospitals grew from $342,291 in April 1992, when the program was beginning, to $2,332,127 for August 1992, according to a January study by the Legislative Budget Board. Total payments to those facilities during the budget year that ended Aug. 31 approached $70 million, according to preliminary tallies by the state Health Department. In September, after state Medicaid officials clamped down on the program and new state laws went into effect, the state was charged for only one patient at a cost of $1,467. A number of the hospitals receiving payments were the same ones that paid settlements to the state last year after being accused of bilking the Crime Victims' Compensation Fund. State investigators said they were stunned by the Medicaid program's rapidly growing costs, which came during the probe into those other hospital abuses."

"A Department of Human Services sampling of claims during a three-month period earlier this year showed 35 percent of the cases didn't qualify for all of the state payments they received, either because the child should not have been admitted at all or because the child stayed in the hospital longer than necessary. It also found nearly half of the children admitted during the period were diagnosed as suffering from "major depression disorder," with the second-highest number being admitted for "disturbance of conduct," such as running away from home, truancy from school, breaking into a home or using a weapon in a fight. Health Department records show that in the most recent fiscal year, the early screening program paid for 3,339 people under age 21 to be treated in private psychiatric hospitals.

That included 205 children from ages 1 to 5. An additional 2,272 children ages 6 to 14 were admitted to the hospitals under the program."

"State officials acknowledge that although children under age 10 may require psychiatric care, it is rare that they would require inpatient psychiatric treatment. "I can think of almost no circumstances where a 2-year-old should be in a psychiatric hospital. That's been a problem and I think the state recognizes that," said Dr. Mike McKinney, a former state representative who is now medical director of National Heritage Insurance Co., which contracts with the state to administer Medicaid payments."

"September, the state tightened its regulations and the number of children admitted to psychiatric hospitals slowed to a trickle. ... April 1992 was the earliest that the department maintained records.

Period.................................Number of clients......Cost...
April 1992-August 1992....................342............$ 6,149,181..
September 1992-August 1993........3,339...........$ 69,460,334..
September 1993.....................................1....................$ 1,467.."

5. Whether, in the best interests of morality, humanity, Constitutionality and equal justice, this Court must review, revise and reverse all Decisions based upon the Four Principles in Question 1, regardless of the volume of work involved.

LIST OF PARTIES

[ ] All parties appear in the caption of the case on the cover page.

[X] All parties **do not** appear in the caption of the case on the cover page. A list of all parties to the proceeding in the court whose judgment is the subject of this petition is as follows:

1. Donald L. Baker, **among a class of citizens with mental illnesses and other disabilities damaged by this Court's Decisions**

2. The Supreme Court of the United States, in its various incarnations, from the present day back to at least Scott v. Sanford (Dred Scott, 1856)

TABLE OF AUTHORITIES CITED

(Note: FRCP requires index of page numbers here where each authority occurs in document)

Constitutional Provisions

Laws Cited

Cases Cited

Cases by title

Addington v. Texas, 441 U.S. 418 (1979)

Albertson's v. Kirkingburg, 527 U.S. 555 (1999)

Barefoot v. Estelle, 463 U.S. 880 (1983)

Brown v. Board of Education (1954)

Buck v. Bell - 274 U.S. 200 (1927)

City of New Orleans v. Warner 176 US 92 (1899)

City of New York 147 US 72 (1893)

Daubert v. Merrell Dow Pharmaceuticals, Inc., 509 U.S. 579 (1993)

Other

Articles and books by author

Akin, John Warren, 2009, Inherited Realities: Eugenics, Oliver Wendell Holmes, Jr., and *Buck v. Bell*, *The Tower*, Vol 1, Number 2, Spring 2009

Alexander, George J., 1997, International Human Rights Protection Against Psychiatric Political Abuses, 37 Santa Clara L. Rev. 387 (1997)

Antonius D, 2014, Behavioral health symptoms associated with chronic traumatic encephalopathy: a critical review of the literature and recommendations for treatment and research, J Neuropsychiatry Clin Neurosci. 2014 Fall;26(4):313-22

Appelbaum, P.S., 1984, The Supreme Court looks at psychiatry, Am. J. Psychiatry, 141(7):827-35, July 1984

Baguley, IJ, 2006, Aggressive behavior following brain injury: How common is common?, J Head Trauma Rehabil, 2006, Jan-Feb, 21(1):45-46

Bay, E et al., 2004, Chronic stress conditions do explain posttraumatic brain injury depression, Res Theory Nurs Pract, 2004 Summer-Fall, 18(2-3);213-28

Bay, E & Donders, J, 2008, Risk factors for depressive symptoms after mild-to-moderate traumatic brain injury, Brain Inj, Mar 2008, 22(3):233-41

Beecher-Monas, Erica, 2003, The Epistemology of Prediction: Future Dangerousness Testimony and Intellectual Due Process, Washington and Lee Law Review, Volume 60 | Issue 2, 3-1-2003

Bierer, LM, et al., 2003, Abuse and neglect in childhood: relationship to personality disorder diagnoses, CNS Spectr. 2003 Oct;8(10):737-54

Bogner J, Pilot study of traumatic brain injury and alcohol misuse among service members, Brain Inj. 2015, 29(7-8):905-14

Boodman, Sandra, 1992, Ads for Psychiatric Hosptials Come Under Attack, The Washington Post, May 08, 1992

Briere J, & Elliott DM, 2003, Prevalence and psychological sequelae of self-reported childhood physical and sexual abuse in a general population sample of men and women, Child Abuse Negl. 2003 ct;27(10):1205-22

Brown, Katherine & Erin Murphy, *Falling Through the Cracks: The Quebec Mental Health System,* 45 MCGILL L.J. 1037, 1062 (2000)

Deneen, Sally, 1988, Complaints about psychiatric hospitals rise, August 19, 1988, Sun-Sentinel, Florida

DeKosky, ST, 2013, Acute and chronic traumatic encephalopathies: pathogenesis and biomarkers, Nat Rev Neurol. 2013 Apr;9(4):192-200

~~Douglass, Frederick, 1845, Narrative of the Life of Frederick Douglass, an American Slave, Elegant Books, Anti-Slavery Office, Boston.~~

Draper, K, et al., 2007, Psychosocial and emotional outcomes 10 years following traumatic brain injury, J Head Trauma Rehabil, Sept 2007, 22(5):278-87

Edwards VJ, et al., 2003, Relationship between multiple forms of childhood maltreatment and adult mental health in community respondents: results from the adverse childhood experiences study, Am J Psychiatry. 2003 Aug;160(8):1453-60

Erlinder,C. Peter, 2003, Essay: Of Rights Lost and Rights Found: The Coming Restoration of the Right to a Jury Trial in Minnesota Civil Commitment Proceedings, 29 Wm. Mitchell L. Rev. 1269

Fazel et al., 2012, Use of risk assessment instruments to predict violence and antisocial behavior in 73 samples involving 24,827 people: systematic review and meta-analysis, British Medical Journal, 2012;345:e4692.

~~Fisher, William H., Jeffrey L. Geller and John A. Padiani, 2009, The Changing Role of the State Psychiatric Hospital, Health Affairs, May/June 2009 vol. 28 no. 3 676-684~~

Fitzsimons, GJ and B. Shiv, 2001, Nonconscious and Contaminative Effects of Hypothetical Questions on Subsequent Decision Making, JOURNAL OF CONSUMER RESEARCH, Inc., Vol. 28, September 2001, pp 224-38

Goodman LA, et al., 2001, Recent victimization in women and men with severe mental illness: prevalence and correlates, J Trauma Stress. 2001 Oct;14(4):615-32

Gottstein, James B., 2008, Involuntary commitment and forced psychiatric drugging in the trial courts: rights violations as a matter of course, Alaska Law Review, Vol. 25:51-105

Gray, Benjamin, 2009, Psychiatry and Oppression: A Personal Account of Compulsory Admission and Medical Treatment, Schizophrenia Bulletin vol. 35 no. 4 pp. 661–663, 2009

Grodin, Michael and George Annas, 2007, Physicians and torture: lessons from the Nazi doctors, Int'l Review of the Red Cross, Volume 89 Number 867 September 2007

Hays JR, The role of Addington v Texas on involuntary civil commitment, Psychol Rep. 1989 Dec;65(3 Pt 2):1211-5

Harlow, K, 2007, Applying the Reasonable Person Standard to Psychosis: How Tort Law Unfairly Burdens Adults with Mental Illness, Ohio State Law Journal, 68:1733-60

Hoge, CW, 2008, Mild traumatic brain injury in U.S. Soldiers returning from Iraq, N Engl J Med, Jan 2008, 358(5):453-63

Hortas, Laura E., *Asylum Protection for the Mentally Disabled: How the Evolution of Rights for the Mentally Ill in the United States Created a "Social Group,"* 20 CONN. J. INT'L L. 155, 159 (2004).

Ilie, G, et al., Suicidality, bullying and other conduct and mental health correlates of traumatic brain injury in adolescents, PLoS One. 2014 Apr 15;9(4)

Jorge RE, 2015, Mood disorders, Handb Clin Neurol. 2015;128:613-31

Kaufer DI, 2015, Neurobehavioral assessment, Continuum (Minneap Minn). 2015 Jun;21(3 Behavioral Neurology and Neuropsychiatry):597-612

Kerr, Peter, 1992, Government review finds 64% of psychiatric hospital stays aren't needed, New York Times News Service April 29, 1992,

Kilburn, KH and JC Thornton, 1995, Protracted Neurotoxicity from Chlordane Sprayed to Kill Termites, Environmental Health Perspectives, Volume 103, Number 7-8, July-August 1995, pp. 690-94

Kindregan, Charles P., 1966, Sixty Years of Compulsory Eugenic Sterilization: Three Generations of Imbeciles and the Constitution of the United States, Chicago-Kent Law Rev., Vol 43(2):123-143, 1966

Krauss, Daniel A., Joel D. Lieberman, and Jodi Olson, 2004, The Effects of Rational and Experiential Information Processing of Expert Testimony in Death Penalty Cases, Behav. Sci. Law 22: 801–822 (2004)

Laden, Vicki A. and Gregory Schwartz, 2000 Psychiatric Disabilities, the Americans with Disabilities Act, and the New Workplace Violence Account, *BERKELEY JOURNAL OF EMPLOYMENT & LABOR LAW* [Vol. 21:246-270, 2000

Langel, et al., 2003, Psychiatric commitment – patients perspectives, Med Law. 2003;22(1):39-53

Laskowski, RA, et al., Chapter 4 Pathophysiology of Mild TBI Implications for Altered Signaling Pathways, Kobeissy FH, editor. Brain Neurotrauma: Molecular, Neuropsychological, and Rehabilitation Aspects. Boca Raton (FL): CRC Press/Taylor & Francis; 2015

Lombardo, Paul A., 2002, "The American Breed": Nazi Eugenics and the Origins of the Pioneer Fund, Albany Law Review, Vol. 65, No. 3, 2002

Loo, Hon. Cynthia, 2007, Predicting Violence in the Mentally Ill, The Criminal Docket, Criminal Justice Section of the Los Angeles County Bar Association, July 2007, Volume II, Number 2

Lyons, Richard D., 1984, How release of mental patients began, NY Times, Oct 20, 1984

Miller, Sarah L. and Stanley L. Brodsky, 2011, Risky Business: Addressing the Consequences of Predicting Violence, J Am Acad Psychiatry Law 39:396–401, 2011

Mariner, Wendy K., JD, LLM, MPH, George J. Annas JD, MPH, and Leonard H. Glantz JD, 2005, Jacobson v Massachusetts : It's Not Your Great-Great-Grandfather's Public Health Law, April 2005, Vol 95, No. 4 | American Journal of Public Health

MacArthur Violence Risk Assessment Study, August 1996 Executive Summary, American Psychology-Law Society, Division 41, American Psychological Association, Fall 1996 Vol. 16, No. 3

McGuan, Elizabeth A. (2009) "New Standards for the Involuntary Commitment of the Mentally Ill: "Danger" Redefined," *Marquette Elder's Advisor: Vol. 11: Iss. 1, Article 10.* Available at: http://scholarship.law.marquette.edu/elders/vol11/iss1/10

McFarlane A, Schrader G, Bookless C, Browne D., 2006, Prevalence of victimization, posttraumatic stress disorder and violent behaviour in the seriously mentally ill, Aust N Z J Psychiatry. 2006 Nov-Dec;40(11-12):1010-5

McKee AC, 2013, The spectrum of disease in chronic traumatic encephalopathy, Brain. 2013 Jan;136(Pt 1):43-64

McNally, RJ, et al., 2003, Does early psychological intervention promote recovery from posttraumatic stress?, *Psychological Science in the Public Interest,* vol. 4, no. 2, November 2003, pp. 45-79

Mehler, Barry, 1987, 'Eliminating the Inferior: American and Nazi Sterilization Programs,' *Science for the People* (Nov-Dec 1987) pp. 14-18.

Mohr, Wanda K., 1998, Experiences of patients hospitalized during the Texas mental health scandal, Perspectives in Psychiatric Care, Vol 34, 1998

Monahan, John, circa 1981. The Clinical Prediction of Violent Behavior, 1995 softcover ed., Jason Aronson, Inc., Northvale, NJ & London, 134 p., over 200 references

Monahan, John, 6-1-2000, Violence Risk Assessment: Scientific Validity and Evidentiary Admissibility, Washington and Lee Law Rev, Article 8, 57(3):901-918

Monahan, et al., 2001-2005, MacArthur Risk Assessment Study

Moore RD, 2015, Neurophysiological correlates of persistent psycho-affective alterations in athletes with a history of concussion, Brain Imaging Behav. 2015 Nov 5

Nadler, Art, 1998, Several claim they've been hospitalized against their will, Las Vegas Sun, Jan 24, 1998

Naef, Andrea Kloehn, 2012, Toyota Motor Manufacturing v. Williams: A Case of Carpal Tunnel Syndrome Weakens the Grip of the Americans with Disabilities Act, Pepperdine Law Review, Volume 31 | Issue 2 Article 5, p 575

~~Payer, Lynn, 1992, Disease- Mongers: How Doctors, Drug Companies, and Insurers Are Making You Feel Sick, John Wiley & Sons, Inc., 1992, pp. 234-235~~

Perlin, Micheal L., 1991, Competency, Deinstitutionalization, And Homelessness: A Story Of Marginalization, 28 Hous. L. Rev. 63

Perlin, Michael L, *Morality & Pretextuality, Psychiatry and Law: Of "Ordinary Common Sense," Heuristic Reasoning, and Cognitive Dissonance,* 19 BULL. AM. ACAD. PSYCHIATRY & L. 131 (1991)

Perlin, Michael L., 1993/1994, The ADA and Persons with Mental Disabilities: Can Sanist Attitudes Be Undone?, Journal of Law and Health, 1993/1994 Symposium, 8 JLHEALTH 15, 27p

Pfeiffer, David, 1994, Eugenics and Disability Discrimination, Disability & Society, 9 (4), 1994, pages 481-99

Rappaport, Richard G., MD, 2006, Losing Your Rights: Complications of Misdiagnosis, J Am Acad Psychiatry Law 34:4:436-438 (December 2006)

Roberson, Shawn. 2009. Interrogations and False Confessions – What Attorneys Should Know From the Social Sciences. The Gauntlet, Law Journal of the Oklahoma Criminal Defense Lawyers Association, Spring 2009:57-71

Saleptsi E, et al., 2004, Negative and positive childhood experiences across developmental periods in psychiatric patients with different diagnoses - an explorative study, BMC Psychiatry. 2004 Nov 26;4:40

Sansone RA, et al., 2005, Childhood trauma and employment disability, Int J Psychiatry Med. 2005;35(4):395-404

Sansone RA, et al., 2006, Childhood trauma, borderline personality symptomatology, and psychophysiological and pain disorders in adulthood, Psychosomatics. 2006 Mar-Apr;47(2):158-62

Scherer, Rachel A., *Toward a Twenty-First Century Civil Commitment Statute: A Legal, Medical, and Policy Analysis of Preventative Outpatient Treatment,* 4 IND. HEALTH L. REV. 361, 382-83 (2007)

Scherr, Alexander, 2003, Daubert & Danger: The "Fit" of Expert Predictions in Civil Commitments, 55 HASTINGS L.J. 1, 2, 17–18 (2003).

Scurich, NI, 2009, The effects of framing and actuarial risk probabilities on involuntary civil commitment decisions, a thesis presented to the faculty of the graduate school, University of Southern California, in partial fulfillment of the requirements for the Degree Master of Arts (Psychology)

Seel RT, 2003, Depression after traumatic brain injury, Arch Phys Med Rehabil, Feb 2003, 84(2):177-84

Sileo, Chi Chi, 1994, Rip-off depress mental health care – fraud in psychiatric hospital practices, Insight on the News, Jan 24, 1994

Smith, Mark, 1991, PROFITABLE ADDICTIONS/Captured and held against will/Some private hospitals prey on patients with insurance, Houston Chronicle 09/09/1991

Smith, Mark, 1992, Profitable Addictions/Abuses in mental health programs are pinpointed, Houston Chronicle. 04/29/1992, Section A, p 1,2

Smith, Mark, 1993a, Profitable Addictions/Doctor who triggered probe claims he's scapegoat, Houston Chronicle, 07/18/1993 Section State, p 1,2

Smith, Mark, 1993b, State probes psychiatric care of youth Morales checks into legality of expensive hospitalizations, Houston Chronicle, 11/21/1993

Smith, Mark, & Cindy Rugeley, 1993, State probes psychiatric care of youth Morales checks into legality of expensive hospitalizations, SUN 11/21/1993 HOUSTON CHRONICLE, Section A, Page 1, 2 STAR Edition

Smith, Mark, 1997, "Few doctors lost licenses over scandal/Psychiatric hospitals accused of filling beds `at any cost'", Houston Chronicle, MON 03/24/1997 HOUSTON CHRONICLE, Section A, Page 1, 3 STAR Edition,

Stéfan A, 2016, What are the disruptive symptoms of behavioral disorders after traumatic brain injury? A systematic review leading to recommendations for good practices, Ann Phys Rehabil Med. 2016 Jan 4, [Epub ahead of print]

Stein TD, 2014, Chronic traumatic encephalopathy: a spectrum of neuropathological changes following repetitive brain trauma in athletes and military personnel, Alzheimers Res Ther. 2014 Jan 15;6(1):4

Stern, Alexandra Minna, 2005, "Sterilized in the name of public health: Race, Immigration, and Reproductive Control in Modern California", American Journal of Public Health | July 2005, Vol 95, No. 7, 1128-1138

Sundman M, et al., 2015, Neuroimaging assessment of early and late neurobiological sequelae of traumatic brain injury: implications for CTE, Front Neurosci. 2015 Sep 24(9):334

Teicher MH, et al., 2006, Sticks, stones, and hurtful words: relative effects of various forms of childhood maltreatment

Teplin LA, McClelland GM, Abram KM, Weiner DA, Crime victimization in adults with severe mental illness: comparison with the National Crime Victimization Survey, Arch Gen Psychiatry. 2005 Aug;62(8):911-21

Tolson, Mike, 2004. Effect of "Dr. Death" and his testimony lingers; Doctor's effect on justice lingers/Testified in many death row cases; By Mike Tolson, June 17, 2004, Houston Chronicle

Torrey, EF, 1995, Jails and prisons - America's new mental hospitals. *Am J Public Health*, 85, 1611-1613

Torrey, EF, 1997, Out of the Shadows: Confronting America's Mental Illness Crisis, New York: John Wiley & Sons

Usahacharoenporn, Proud, 2011, E.P. v. Alaska Psychiatric Institute: The Evolution of Involuntary Civil Commitments from Treatment to Punishment, Alaska Law Rev., 28(1):189-216

Vanderploeg, RD, 2007, Long-term morbidities following self-reported mild traumatic brain injury, J Clin Exp Neuropsychol. 2007 Aug, 29(6):585-98

Weyer JC, 2013, Pain and mild traumatic brain injury: the implications of pain severity on emotional and cognitive functioning, Brain Inj. 2013;27(10):1134-40

Windom, CS, 1999, Posttraumatic stress disorder in abused and neglected children grown up, Am J Psychiatry. 1999 Aug;156(8):1223-9

Wong GK, 2014, Neuropsychiatric disturbance after aneurysmal subarachnoid hemorrhage, J Clin Neurosci. 2014 Oct;21(10):1695-8

Web sites by author or title

Baker, DL, Oct 2014, Origins and Effects of SCOTUS Mental Health Rulings: A Reading List, independent.academia.edu/DonaldLBaker/,

~~Buck v. Bell, Origins of Eugenics and Influence of Eugenics, Claude Moore Health Sciences Library, http://exhibits.hsl.virginia.edu/eugenics~~

Buck v. Bell - Wikipedia, the free encyclopedia http://en.wikipedia.org/wiki/Buck_v._Bell

Can the US Supreme Court Reverse Its Own Decisions, http://wiki.answers.com/Q/Can_the_US_Supreme_Court_reverse_its_own_decisions

Claude Moore Health Sciences Library, 2004, Origins of Eugenics, http://exhibits.hsl.virginia.edu/eugenics/2-origins/

Claude Moore Health Sciences Library, 2004, Buck v. Bell - Eugenics_ Three Generations, No Imbeciles_ Virginia, Eugenics & Buck v. Bell, http://exhibits.hsl.virginia.edu/eugenics/3-buckvbell/

Claude Moore Health Sciences Library, 2004, Influence | Eugenics: Three Generations, No Imbeciles: Virginia, Eugenics & Buck v. Bell, U. of Virginia, http://exhibits.hsl.virginia.edu/eugenics/4-influence/

Claude Moore Health Sciences Library, 2004, Carrie Buck Revisited | Eugenics: Three Generations, No Imbeciles, U. of Virginia, http://exhibits.hsl.virginia.edu/eugenics/5-epilogue/

Colb, Sherry F., Aug 10, 2011, Armed and Crazy: Should Mentally Ill People Be Permitted to Own Firearms?, Justia.com

Cooper, Alexia and Erica L. Smith, Nov 2011, PATTERNS & TRENDS, Homicide Trends in the United States, 1980-2008, U.S. Bureau of Justice Statistics, NCJ 236018

Electric Shocks Are Inhumane And Barbaric, http://www.cchrflorida.org/blog/electric-shocks-areinhumane-and-barbaric/ and http://www.youtube.com/watch?v=RlJ10qnrfl4&

Gems, David, 1999, Review Essay: Politically Correct Eugenics, Theoretical Medicine and Bioethics (1999) 20, 199-211, http://www.ucl.ac.uk/~ucbtdag/bioethics/writings/eugenics.html

Gottstein, James B., Mental Health Recovery Stories: Jim Gottstein, Alaska Mental Health Consumer Web, http://akmhcweb.org/recovery/jgrec.htm

Gottstein, JB, 2002, Psychiatry: Force of Law, Nov 2002, PsychRights, Law Project for Psychiatric Rights, psychrights.org

History of Psychiatric Insitutions, 2013, Wikipedia, http://en.wikipedia.org/wiki/History_of_psychiatric_institutions,

Influence - Eugenics_ Three Generations, No Imbeciles_ Virginia, Eugenics & Buck v. Bell, © 2004 Claude Moore Health Sciences Library, http://exhibits.hsl.virginia.edu/eugenics/4-influence/

Joseph DeJarnette, http://en.wikipedia.org/wiki/Joseph_DeJarnette

Lyons, RD, 1984, How Release of Mental Patient Began, New York Times, Oct 30, 1984, http://www.nytimes.com/1984/10/30/science/how-release-of-me...

McCarthy, Kara, 2011, Nov 16, "HOMICIDES FALL TO LOWEST RATE IN FOUR DECADES", U.S. Bureau of Justice Statistics, http://www.bjs.gov/content/pub/press/htus8008pr.cfm

Medical Encyclopedia: Post-traumatic stress disorder, http://www.lnlmnih.gov/medlineplus/print/ency/article/000925.htm

Moffic, H. Steven, 2013, M.D., The rise and fall and rise again of Magellan, Sept 30, 2013, http://www.behavioral.net/blogs/h-steven-moffic/rise-and-fall-and-rise-again-magellan

Mostert, Mark P., 2002, Useless Eaters: Disability as Genocidal Marker in Nazi Germany, 2002, http://www.catholicculture.org/culture/library/view.cfm?id=7019&repos=1&subrepos=0&searchid=1146140 © 2013 Trinity Communications

National Council on Disability, 2003, The Americans with Disabilities Act Policy Brief Series: No. 7 The Impact of the Supreme Court's ADA Decisions on the Rights of Persons With Disabilities, February 25, 2003, http://www.ncd.gov/newsroom/publications/2003/decisionsimpact.htm

Nilsson, Kevin, circa 2000, Eugenics: A Historical Analysis, http://campus.udayton.edu/~hume/Eugenics/eugenics.htm

Olberg, Becky, 2011, The Abuse of Psychiatric Detention and Its Complications, http://www.healthyplace.com/blogs/borderline/2011/02/the-abu...

~~Origins of Eugenics - Eugenics_ Three Generations, No Imbeciles_ Virginia, Eugenics & Buck v. Bell, © 2004 Claude Moore Health Sciences Library, http://exhibits.hsl.virginia.edu/eugenics/2-origins/~~

~~Petrila, John & Hallie Fader Towe, 2010, Information Sharing in Criminal Justice – Mental Health Collaborations: Working with HIPAA and other Privacy Laws, U.S. DOJ Bureau of Justice Administration & Council of State Governments Justice Center, 2010, 46p, https://www.bja.gov/Publications/CSG_CJMH_Info_Sharing.pdf~~

~~Psychiatric Hospitals market report, Highbeam Business, http://business.highbeam.com/industry-reports/business/psychiatric-hospitals~~

Rubin, Nilmini Gunaratne, 2012, A crime against motherhood - Involuntary sterilization was a horrifying exercise in genetic engineering, Los Angeles Times, May 13, 2012, http://articles.latimes.com/2012/may/13/opinion/la-oe-rubin-eugenics-mothers-day-20120513

Skinner v. Oklahoma, http://en.wikipedia.org/wiki/Skinner_v._Oklahoma Wikipedia

Spiegel, Alix, November 12, 2012 4:00 AM, Struggle For Smarts? How Eastern And Western Cultures Tackle Learning, NPR Morning Edition, http://www.npr.org/blogs/health/2012/11/12/164793058/struggle...

Stevens, Lawrence, J.D., Unjustified psychiatric commitment in the U.S.A., http://www.antipsychiatry.org/unjustif.htm

Thomas, Alexandar, 1998, Ronald Reagan and the Commitment of the Mentally Ill: Capital, Interest Groups, and the Eclipse of Social Policy, Electronic Journal of Sociology (1998), http://sociology.org/content/vol003.004/thomas_d.html

"Three Generations of Imbeciles"?, http://www.facinghistory.org/three-generations-imbeciles, From Race and Membership in American History: The Eugenics Movement, Chapter 6

Turgeon, Carolyn, Jan 2005, Interview: Stephen V. Manley, Judge, Mental Health Treatment Court, Santa Clara County, California; http://www.courtinnovation.org/research/stephen-v-manley-judge-mental-healthtreatment-court-santa-clara-county-california

USCCR, 2000, "Sharing the Dream: Is the ADA Accommodating All?", U.S. Commission on Civil Rights, Oct 2000, Chapter 5, Psychiatric Disabilities and the ADA, Usccr.gov-pubs-ada-ch5.htm – web page, www.usccr.gov/pubs/ada/main.htm

~~Van Ornum, William Eugenics: Beware of History Repeating Itself, American Mental Health Foundation, http://americanmentalhealthfoundation.org/2013/02/eugenics-beware-of-history-repeating-itself/, Feb 17, 2013~~

Virginia Eugenics, circa 2008, http://www.uvm.edu/~lkaelber/eugenics/VA/VA.html

Wikipedia, 2013, Political abuse of psychiatry in the Soviet Union, http://en.wikipedia.org/wiki/Political_abuse_of_psychiatry_in_...

IN THE
SUPREME COURT OF THE UNITED STATES
A DIRECT PETITION FOR REVERSAL OF DECISIONS

Petitioner respectfully prays the Court to reconsider for revision and reversal various past decisions regarding eugenic sterilization, mental illness and disability rights.

OPINIONS BELOW

[X] For cases from **the Supreme Court of the United States and other courts**, most long published, including but not limited to:

1. Scott v. Sanford, 60 U.S. 393 (1856)

2. City of New York 147 US 72 (1893)

3. Plessy v. Ferguson, 163 U.S. 537 (1896)

4. City of New Orleans v. Warner 176 US 92 (1899)

5. Jacobson v Massachusetts, 197 US 11 (1905)

6. Gould v. Gould, Supp Ct of Conn (1905)

7. Osborn v. Thomson, 185 App. Div. 902, 171 N.Y. Supp. 1094 (1918)

8. Buck v. Bell - 274 U.S. 200 (1927)

9. Whitney v. California, 274 U.S. 357 (1927) 2

10. Skinner v. Oklahoma 316 U.S. 535 (1942)

11. Brown v. Board of Education (1954)

12. Robinson v. California, 370 U.S. 660 (1962)

13. In re Gault, 387 U.S. 1, 87 S.Ct. 1428, 18 L.Ed. 2d 527 (1966)

14. Thornton v. Corcoran, 132 U. S. App. D. C. 232, 407 F. 2d 695, (1969)

15. Winship, 397 U.S. 358 (1970)

16. Lessard v. Schmidt, 349 F. Supp. 1078 – Dist. Court, ED Wisconsin (1972)

17. O'Connor v. Donaldson, 422 U.S. 563 (1975)

18. Madrigal v Quilligan, 9th Cir, 639 F.2d 789 (1978)

19. Addington v. Texas, 441 U.S. 418 (1979)

20. Rennie v. Klein, 476 F. Supp. 1294, 1299-1300 (D.N.J. 1979)

21. Estelle v. Smith, 451 U.S. 454 (1981)

22. Jones v. United States, 463 U. S. 354 (1983)

23. Barefoot v. Estelle, 463 U.S. 880 (1983)

24. Rogers v. Okin, 738 F2d 1 Nos. 79-1648, 79-1649, U.S. Court of Appeals, First Circuit (1984)

25. Washington v. Harper, 494 U.S. 210 (1990)

26. Foucha v. Louisiana, 504 U.S. 71 (1992)

27. Heller v. Doe, 509 U. S. 312 (1993)

28. Daubert v. Merrell Dow Pharmaceuticals, Inc., 509 U.S. 579 (1993)

29. Kansas v. Hendricks, 521 U.S. 346 (1997)

30. Sutton v. United Airlines, 527 U.S. 471 (1999)

31. Murphy v.United Parcel Service, 527 U.S. 516 (1999)

32. Albertson's v. Kirkingburg, 527 U.S. 555 (1999)

33. Toyota v. Williams, 534 U.S. 184, 202 (2002)

34. Tennessee v. Lane (02-1667) 541 U.S. 509 (2004), 315 F.3d 680

35. United States v. Georgia et al, No. 04-1203 (2006)

36. United States v. Parker, No. 07-6239 (10th Cir., January 9, 2009)

37. U.S.A v. Stone, et al., Fed. Dist. Ct. MIED, 2:10-cr-20123-VAR-PJK, (3/27/2012)

38. Friedman v. Highland Park, 7th Cir #14-3091, 784 F.3d 406, SCOTUS #15-133 (2015)

JURISDICTION

[X] For cases from **the Supreme Court of the United States:**

[N/A] No petition for rehearing was timely filed in my case.
[N/A] A timely petition for rehearing was denied by the United States Court of Appeals on the following date: ,

The jurisdiction of this Court is invoked under 28 U. S. C. § 1254(1), the authority of this Court to review its own decisions [42] [43] [44] [45], including evidence that this Court has overlooked or has since come to light [46] [47] [48] [49] [50] [51], and this Court's Constitutional

---

[42] Can the US Supreme Court Reverse Its Own Decisions, http://wiki.answers.com/Q/Can_the_US_Supreme_Court_reverse_its_own_decisions

[43] City of New York 147 US 72 (1893) (cited in 2):

"(3) That if the court below neglects or refuses to make a finding one way or the other as to the existence of a material fact which has been established by uncontradicted evidence, or if it finds such a fact when not supported by any evidence whatever and an exception be taken, the question may be brought up for review in that particular."

[44] City of New Orleans v. Warner 176 US 92 (1899) (cited in 2): Court overlooked material fact/evidence.

[45] Brown v. Board of Education (1954) reversing Plessey v. Ferguson (1896) (cited in 2).

[46] Tolson, Mike, 2004, Effect of "Dr. Death" and his testimony lingers, Houston Chronicle, June 17, 2004, citing the inherent conflict of interest and corruption in the unscientific testimony of a man upon which the Court relied heavily in Barefoot v. Estelle (1983)

[47] Roberson, Shawn, 2009, Interrogations and False Confessions – What Attorneys Should Know From the Social Sciences, The Gauntlet, Spring 2009:57-71, describing the high propensity for innocent and harmless people to incriminate themselves without counsel in criminal cases, especially when hampered by mental impairment such as intoxication, lack of maturity (minors), intellectual disabilities and mental illness, much less in psychiatric examinations where no counsel is allowed and the examiner frequently labors under the moral hazard of interviewing for his or her own future patients and income producers; also noting that interrogators who are more confident:

"With very few exceptions, research has not supported the conclusion that law enforcement professionals are effective in detecting deception (including mental health professionals). Kassin, Meissner & Norwick (2005) assessed the ability of college students and police investigators to accurately predict true versus false confessions of inmates on videotape. The results indicated that *neither* group was effective. The hit rate for accuracy was around 50%, which is not better than chance levels. [note that historically psychiatric clinical predictions of violent behavior have been even less accurate, at right 1 time in 3]

"Kassin & Fong (1999) went a step further, having subjects commit a mock crime (or not) and then sign a *Miranda* waiver and maintain their innocence during a videotaped interrogation. Next, two groups, either trained in the Reid Technique or not, viewed the tapes. The results indicated that naïve subjects actually outperformed those with Reid training (although both were around chance levels). However, the Reid training subjects were more confident and cited more reasons for their decisions. The implications being that the Reid technique training did not improve detecting deception, but *increased the belief in the subject that it did.*" ... [implies that a psychiatrist's training with the Diagnostic and Statistical Manual and feeling of "special insight into the human mind" can produce overconfidence of a correct evaluation of dangerousness, even when it is wrong, thus producing a falsely confident "expert witness", upon which a judge or jury falsely depends]

"In an ingenious study with real world implications, Russano, Meissner, Narchet, & Kassin (2005) induced unknowing college students to "cheat" with a confederate during an experiment. Naturally, some did and others did not. However, all subjects were then threatened by the researcher with the professor being contacted and the potential ramifications. Various groups were then exposed to specific interrogation tactics, such as minimization and/or specifically offering a "deal" for a confession. As hypothesized, diagnosticity was greatly reduced with these techniques. When the tactic of minimization was used in conjunction with a "deal," nearly half of the innocent college students falsely confessed to having cheated." [Implies that psychiatric evaluations can also be rigged to produce false results]

[48] Miller, Sarah L. and Stanley L. Brodsky, 2011, Risky Business: Addressing the Consequences of Predicting Violence, J Am Acad Psychiatry Law 39:396–401, 2011,

"Adversarial allegiance, or the tendency to lean in favor of the hiring side, is an additional risk.[15] Further, confidence or level of experience may influence the consequences to the predictor. In one prospective study, clinicians were generally confident in their risk assessments, although some findings suggest that higher levels of confidence were associated with lower accuracy in predicting future aggression.[22]"

[49] Monahan, et al., circa 2001-2005, The MacArthur Violence Risk Assessment Study,

citing the vast inaccuracy of the clinical prediction of violent behavior, relied upon in such cases as Barefoot (1983), as compared to statistical measures, such as the presence of past violent behavior and substance abuse, which demonstrates statistical validity for predicting only the most violent and the most harmless, with a broad gray area in between

responsibility to correct the severe and extreme injustices and moral hazards caused by its decisions in mental health, disability and eugenics issues.

---

[50] Stern, Alexandra Minna, 2005, Sterilized in the Name of Public Health, Am J of Pub Health, 95(7):1128-38, demonstrating widespread sterilization under eugenics laws, often without knowledge or consent of mostly poor, colored and foreign-born, including unwed mothers and masturbators.

[51] Rubin, Nilmini Gunaratne, 2012, A crime against motherhood - Involuntary sterilization was a horrifying exercise in genetic engineering, Los Angeles Times, May 13, 2012, http://articles.latimes.com/2012/may/13/opinion/la-oe-rubin-eugenics-mothers-day-20120513 , written by the daughter of a foreign-born woman, involuntarily sterilized after giving birth to the daughter in 1972, because the white Doctor claimed, "There are too many colored babies already", a direct result of the 1927 Buck v. Bell Decision.

INTRODUCTION

39. Common principles of human bigotry and oppression run throughout human history and jurisprudence. They support slavery, apartheid, eugenic sterilization, the Nazi Holocaust, civil commitment, racism, sectarianism, sexism, sanism, ablism, sex trafficking, and discrimination of all kinds against innocent and harmless people, differing only in application and degree. If we do not recognize and expose them wherever they exist, they can never be fully defeated. So long as we condone these principles for one last group of people who have done us no harm, none of us are safe.

40. So long as the Highest Court in the Land condones them, our society is not safe.

STATEMENT OF THE CASE

All the way back to Dred Scott

41.   At least as far back as Scott v. Sanford (1856)[52], where the Supreme Court of the United States famously said, "They [negroes] had for more than a century before been regarded as beings of an inferior order, and altogether unfit to associate with the white race either in social or political relations, and so far inferior that they had **no rights which the white man was bound to respect**, and that the negro might justly and lawfully **be reduced to slavery for his benefit**" [emphasis added], has generated and used the afore-mentioned Four Principles of Oppression to define some despised minority as undeserving of the same legal protections and due process of the majority.   In Scott, this Court listed a parade of horribles[53]:

> For if they were so received, and entitled to the privileges and immunities of citizens, it would exempt them from the operation of the special laws and from the police [Page 60 U. S. 417] regulations which they considered to be necessary for their own safety. It would give to persons of the negro race, who were recognised as citizens in any one State of the Union, the right to enter every other State whenever they pleased, singly or in companies, without pass or passport, and without obstruction, to sojourn there as long as they pleased, to go where they pleased at every hour of the day or night without molestation, unless they committed some violation of law for which a white man would be punished; and it would give them the full liberty of speech in public and in private upon all subjects upon which its own citizens might speak; to hold public meetings upon political affairs, and to keep and carry arms wherever they went. And all of this would be done in the face of the subject race of the same color, both free and slaves, and inevitably producing discontent and insubordination among them, and **endangering the peace and safety of the State**. [emphasis added] [Note "to keep and carry arms", not unlike the debate today over registering people with mental

---

[52]   Scott v. Sanford, 60 U.S. 393 (1856)

[53]   Amendments 1 to 10,

illness on government watch lists to keep them from buying and possessing firearms, for the "peace and safety of the State".]

42. Even after Emancipation and the Civil War, when the races were held to be "equal", this Court stated in Plessy v. Ferguson (1896)[54], that "he [Plessy] is not lawfully entitled to the reputation of being a white man", in support of arresting Plessy for insisting on sitting in a whites-only railroad car.

This Court and eugenic sterilization

43. In 1883, Sir Francis Galton, a British statistician, coined the term "eugenics", from the Greek for good breeding, aided somewhat by his cousin Charles Darwin's theory of evolution[55]. This unproven theory held that crime, poverty, moral character and a number of diseases and disabilities could be inherited. At first, eugenicists concentrated on positive eugenics, the promotion of breeding among "superior" human stock. Later, it emphasized weeding out "inferior" stock, with the United States and Germany eugenicists corresponding with and honoring each other while leading the charge [56] [57] [58]. As the German economy collapsed after WWI, both the educated and

---

[54] Plessy v. Ferguson, 163 U.S. 537 (1896)

[55] Nilsson, Kevin, circa 2000, Eugenics: A Historical Analysis, http://campus.udayton.edu/~hume/Eugenics/eugenics.htm

[56] Mehler, Barry, 1987, 'Eliminating the Inferior: American and Nazi Sterilization Programs,' *Science for the People* (Nov-Dec 1987) pp. 14-18.

[57] Lombardo, Paul A., 2002, "The American Breed": Nazi Eugenics and the Origins of the Pioneer Fund, Albany Law Review, Vol. 65, No. 3, 2002

[58] Claude Moore Health Sciences Library, 2004, Origins of Eugenics, http://exhibits.hsl.virginia.edu/eugenics/2-origins/

common people began to accept more and more the elimination of those who could not contribute to it [59].

> "As one Nazi SS doctor explained it, he participated in Auschwitz exterminations 'out of respect for human life.' Just as the physician 'would remove a purulent appendix from a diseased body,' so he was removing degenerates from the 'body of Europe.' The comparison of degenerate humans with cancer cells and disease is recurrent throughout European and American eugenic literature." (Mehler, 1987)

> "Official notions of difference, which would later find their most diabolical expression in the murder of the Jews, were first expressed in state-sanctioned killings of children and adults with a wide range of physical, emotional, and intellectual disabilities. … In May 1939, Hitler ordered the creation of an advisory committee that would pave the way for the widespread killing of children with disabilities." (Mostert, 2002) [The children were killed by starvation, exposure to cold, poisoning, and induced medical complication.]

44. The first U.S. forced sterilization laws were passed in Pennsylvania (1905) and Indiana (1907), directed primarily at persons with epilepsy, mental retardation, and any other condition considered to be morally or physically inferior. Perhaps Gould v. Gould (1905), in which a woman divorced and epileptic claiming the condition had been hidden best expressed the bigotry of the time. Almost completely ignorant of the medical causes of epilepsy, the Judge stated:

> "That epilepsy is a disease of a peculiarly serious and revolting character, tending to weaken mental force, and often descending from parent to child, or entailing upon the offspring of the sufferer some other grave form of nervous malady, is a matter of common knowledge, of which courts will take judicial notice. State v. Main, 69 Conn. 123, 135. One mode of guarding against the perpetuation of epilepsy obviously is to forbid sexual intercourse with those afflicted by it, and to preclude such opportunities for sexual intercourse as marriage furnishes. To impose such a restriction upon the right to contract marriage, if not intrinsically unreasonable, is no invasion of the equality of all men before the law, if it applies equally to all under the same

---

[59] Mostert, Mark P., 2002, Useless Eaters: Disability as Genocidal Marker in Nazi Germany, 2002, http://www.catholicculture.org/culture/library/view.cfm?id=7019&repos=1&subrepos=0&searchid=11461 40 © 2013 Trinity Communications

circumstances who belong to a certain class of persons, which class can reasonably be regarded as one requiring special legislation either for their protection or for the protection from them of the community at large. … The class of persons to whom the statute applies is not one arbitrarily formed to suit its purpose. It is certain and definite. It is a class capable of endangering the health of families and adding greatly to the sum of human suffering. Between the members of this class there is no discrimination, and the prohibitions of the statute cease to operate when, by the attainment of a certain age by one of those whom it affects, the occasion for the restriction is deemed to become less imperative."

45. "Common knowledge" is often just another term for common bigotry, which Judges and States have often used to justify special sanctions against a despised (or feared) and poorly understood minority, as Rev. Martin Luther King surely understood.

46. Harry H. Laughlin, the Director of the Eugenics Record Office at Cold Spring Harbor, NY, and a member of the American Breeders Association, wrote a Model Sterilization Act in 1914. In 1924, Virginia enacted it into law as the Eugenical Sterilization Act, to justify sterilizations of alleged "imbeciles" already taking place at the Virginia State Colony for Epileptics and Feeble Minded. Virginia eugenicists chose a Ms. Carrie Buck, committed to the Colony for being an unwed mother, for a test case. Her mother, suffering from syphilis of unknown origin, was already there, for which reason Virginia had fostered Buck with another family. A nephew of the family raped Buck, after which the family had her committed to the Colony as promiscuous.

47. The proponents of the sterilization law chose Buck's lawyer from among their ranks and ran the cause up through the courts to the U.S. Supreme Court. Her lawyer punted, calling no witnesses and raising no objections to any effect. Harry Laughlin testified against her in the initial trial without ever examining her or any of her family, claiming that she had a mental age of nine and came from a degenerate family. One

"expert" witness against her claimed that she was promiscuous because she passed notes to boy in class. Another claimed that her baby didn't look quite right. In ruling that her eugenic sterilization was legal and Constitutional, Supreme Court Justice Oliver Wendell Holmes famously said, "three generations of imbeciles are enough"[60].

48. But the entire case against her might have fallen apart if any Judge anywhere along the line had simply asked the question, "So, how well did she do in school?" Like many of her time, she advanced to sixth grade, where her work was considered "very good". Later, her daughter Vivian made the honor roll. But despite any injustice it may cause, Judges often refuse to consider any fact or issue that was either not brought up in a lower court or set before them on a silver legal platter. Since it tends to simplify and shorten proceedings, the mere appearance of justice seems to be vastly more important than the actual thing itself. Even 15 years later, in Skinner v. Oklahoma (1945)[61], when this Court had reason to know of Nazi atrocities in the name of eugenics, this Court still had not discovered that Carrie Buck and her daughter had been good students.

> "This Court has sustained such an experiment with respect to an imbecile, a person with definite and observable characteristics, where the condition had persisted through three generations and afforded grounds for the belief that it was transmissible, and would continue to manifest itself in generations to come. *Buck v. Bell,* 274 U. S. 200."

49. Because of Buck v. Bell, many States passed similar laws, which were not repealed until the late 1970s. During which time, states and their agents circumvented most of the due process procedures envisioned by Justice Holmes to protect the innocent

---

[60] Buck v. Bell - 274 U.S. 200 (1927)

[61] Skinner v. Oklahoma 316 U.S. 535 (1942)

[62] [63] [64]. When this Court presumes due process and equal protections, without providing substantive guarantees, either in its Orders or its commentaries on the deficiencies of existing law, the protections from the cruel and unusual punishments of bigotry in Amendments 4, 5, 6, 8, 9, 10 and 14 do not truly exist. Nor do the true freedom of speech of Amendment 1 and right to bear arms of Amendment 2.

50. Under those laws, over 60,000 U.S. citizens, mostly poor and colored, were sterilized against their will into the 1970s, and often without their knowledge or consent. Hitler liked Buck v. Bell so much that he used it to justify and start the Nazi Holocaust with a German sterilization act. In Virginia, authorities took to the hills to round up blacks and poor "white trash", especially those on welfare, to be sterilized without any legal recourse or even knowledge about what was being done to them[65] [66]. Where this Court assumes the arrogance of power and omnipotence, and fails to be humble in its considerations, it becomes more dangerous to society than any mass shooter.

---

[62] Virginia Eugenics http://www.uvm.edu/~lkaelber/eugenics/VA/VA.html

[63] Stern, Alexandra Minna, 2005, "Sterilized in the name of public health: Race, Immigration, and Reproductive Control in Modern California", American Journal of Public Health | July 2005, Vol 95, No. 7, 1128-1138

[64] Rubin, Nilmini Gunaratne, 2012, A crime against motherhood - Involuntary sterilization was a horrifying exercise in genetic engineering, Los Angeles Times, May 13, 2012, http://articles.latimes.com/2012/may/13/opinion/la-oe-rubin-eugenics-mothers-day-20120513

[65] Virginia Eugenics, circa 2008, http://www.uvm.edu/~lkaelber/eugenics/VA/VA.html

[66] Nilsson, Kevin, circa 2000, Eugenics: A Historical Analysis, http://campus.udayton.edu/~hume/Eugenics/eugenics.htm

51.   Thus birthed the Fourth Principle of Oppression, which the Supreme Court of the United States has never seen fit to overturn.

Treatment versus punitive intent

52.   As the effects of Nazi atrocities finally dawned upon U.S. Courts, they moved from allowing widespread sterilization to involuntary forced drugging and commitment. If the State could make a case for providing medical "treatment" without "punitive intent", then what would be cruel and unusual punishment in one case would not be if cast as "treatment" in another[67] [68] [69] [70] [71] [72] [73].

---

[67]   Osborn v. Thomson, 185 App. Div. 902, 171 N.Y. Supp. 1094 (1918)

[68]   In re Gault, 387 U.S. 1, 87 S.Ct. 1428, 18 L.Ed. 2d 527 (1966)

[69]   Lessard v. Schmidt, 349 F. Supp. 1078 – Dist. Court, ED Wisconsin (1972)

"Furthermore, the validity of the *parens patriae* role and the lifting of procedural safeguards in such instances appears to rest in part on the realities of better treatment for the person subjected to incarceration in a civil proceeding. In Kent v. United States, *supra,* the Supreme Court, discussing the issue in the context of juvenile courts, observed:

"The objectives are to provide measures of guidance and rehabilitation for the child and protection for society, not to fix criminal responsibility, guilt and punishment. The State is *parens patriae* rather than prosecuting attorney and judge. But the admonition to function in a `parental' relationship is not an invitation to procedural arbitrariness."

[70]   O'Connor v. Donaldson, 422 U.S. 563 (1975)

[71]   Rogers v. Okin, 738 F2d 1 Nos. 79-1648, 79-1649, U.S. Court of Appeals, First Circuit (1984)

"The Supreme Judicial Court presented this standard after cataloguing known abuses of antipsychotic medication by officials who claimed to act in the incompetent patient's best interests, but who in fact followed agendas of convenience, punishment, and behavior modification. 390 Mass. at 508-09, 458 N.E.2d 308"

[72]   Washington v. Harper, 494 U.S. 210 (1990)

[73]   Kansas v. Hendricks, 521 U.S. 346 (1997)

53. This and lower Courts have also made distinctions between juveniles and the mentally ill. The Courts hold juveniles to be inherently "good" and capable of rehabilitation. Thus it would be cruel and unusual to subject them to the evidentiary and judgment standards of "a preponderance of the evidence" – they deserve the full protection of criminal procedure, even if they are demonstrated to be dangerous to themselves and others.

54. But despite the known medical fact that juvenile brains are not fully formed and are often subject to extreme swings of mood and judgment, people with mental illnesses are depicted in this Court as undeserving of full criminal evidentiary and procedural standards, for the protection of society, due to "the dangerous tendencies of some"[74]. In this society and this Court, profiling by age and race may be forbidden, but despite much lower rates of violence among those with mental illness, profiling by mental illness is upheld.

55. This Court also held in Addington (1979) that while the standard of "beyond a reasonable doubt" was not justified for civil commitment, the standard of "clear and convincing evidence" was somehow superior to "a preponderance" and more protective. There is no evidence that "clear and convincing" has made any difference whatsoever[75].

---

[74] Addington v. Texas, 441 U.S. 418 (1979)

[75] Hays JR, The role of Addington v Texas on involuntary civil commitment, Psychol Rep. 1989 Dec;65(3 Pt 2):1211-5,

"There was no reduction in the rates of commitment as a result of the decision. The proportion of patients committed in **Texas** grew in almost linear fashion during the years 1972-1986. Various economic, sociological, and treatment factors may have more influence on commitment of patients than does a court decision."

Not entirely unreliable

56. By 1981 (Monahan[76]), medical and legal research had shown that violence among those with mental illness is committed by a tiny minority with a previous history of violence and problems with drug or alcohol abuse. Ironically, this Court has held (Robinson v. California, 1962) that an addict cannot be arrested and jailed merely for being an addict, but has to commit the crime of actually using drugs[77]. But since at least the time of Buck v. Bell (1927), those with "mental defects" have held a special place in its heart, like the negroes of 1856 (Scott v. Sanford), subject to confinement and forced "treatment" for the mere potential of "dangerous tendencies" or "danger to self or others", allegedly for their own "benefit".

57. In 1983, this Court decided the case of Barefoot v. Estelle, regarding the penalty trail phase of a Texas prisoner convicted of murder. Despite the fact that Barefoot had no prior history of violent crime[78], a habitual paid "expert witness" for the State of Texas prosecution, Dr. James Grison, otherwise known as "Dr. Death"[79], who evaluated Barefoot only remotely through hypothetical questions, testified that he could with "100% accuracy" predict that Barefoot would be a continuing danger of violence to society, thus ensuring the death sentence. Despite the fact that the American Psychiatric

---

[76] Monahan, John, circa 1981. The Clinical Prediction of Violent Behavior, 1995 softcover ed., Jason Aronson, Inc., Northvale, NJ & London, 134 p., over 200 references

[77] Robinson v. California, 370 U.S. 660, 666 (1962)

[78] Beecher-Monas, Erica, 2003, The Epistemology of Prediction: Future Dangerousness Testimony and Intellectual Due Process, Washington and Lee Law Review, Volume 60 | Issue 2, 3-1-2003

Association entered an amicus brief stating that psychiatrists should not testify in such cases due to the uncertainty of predictions of future violence, and the fact that this Court cited Monahan's research that such prediction were correct only one time in three, this Court asserted that:

> "Nor, despite the view of the American Psychiatric Association supporting petitioner's view, is there any convincing evidence that such testimony is almost entirely unreliable, and that the factfinder and the adversary system will not be competent to uncover, recognize, and take due account of its shortcomings."

58. In any other field of medicine, this would be like saying: "Don't worry about a thing; although your heart surgeon has never seen you or your medical record, he has heard about you through hypothetical questions, and there is no convincing evidence that he is almost entirely unreliable." And like the due process protections against unjust sterilization, subsequent events have shown that the adversarial system fails abysmally in taking those shortcomings into account, if for no other reason than that this Court has declared that lawyers and judges should have little or no say in it[80] [81] [82] [83] [84] [85].

---

[79] Tolson, Mike, 2004. Effect of "Dr. Death" and his testimony lingers; Doctor's effect on justice lingers/Testified in many death row cases; By Mike Tolson, June 17, 2004, Houston Chronicle

[80] Scott v. Sanford, 60 U.S. 393 (1856), in which this Court repeatedly short-circuited any adversarial process in making legislatures the pre-eminent deciders of whether or not slavery was just.

[81] Skinner v. Oklahoma 316 U.S. 535 (1942), referring to Buck v. Bell to justify giving legislatures slack in determining "degrees of evil" that justify differences in equal protection under the law.

[82] O'Connor v. Donaldson, 422 U.S. 563 (1975),

"In light of the wide divergence of medical opinion regarding the diagnosis of and proper therapy for mental abnormalities, that prospect is especially troubling in this area and cannot be squared with the principle that "courts may not substitute for the judgments of legislators their own understanding of the public welfare, but must instead concern themselves with the validity under the Constitution of the methods which the legislature has selected." In re Gault, 387 U.S., at 71 (Harlan, J., concurring and dissenting). Of course, questions regarding the adequacy of procedure and the power of a State to continue particular confinements are ultimately for the courts, aided by expert opinion to the extent that is found helpful. But I am not persuaded that we should abandon the traditional limitations on the scope of judicial review."

[83] Washington v. Harper, 494 U.S. 210 (1990),

""[I]t is less than crystal clear why *lawyers* must be available to identify possible errors in medical judgment." *Walters v. National Association of Radiation Survivors,* 473 U. S. 305, 473 U. S. 330 (1985) (emphasis in original). Given the nature of the decision to be made, we conclude that the provision of an independent lay advisor who understands the psychiatric issues involved is sufficient protection."

"A State may conclude with good reason that a judicial hearing will not be as effective, as continuous, or as probing as administrative review using medical decisionmakers. We hold that due process requires no more. … As we reasoned in *Vitek,* it is only by permitting persons connected with the institution to make these decisions that courts are able to avoid "unnecessary intrusion into either medical or correctional judgments." *Vitek, supra,* 445 U.S. at 445 U. S. 496; *see Turner,* 482 U.S. at 482 U. S. 84-85, 89."

[84] Foucha v. Louisiana, 504 U.S. 71 (1992)

"We noted in Jones that a judicial determination of criminal conduct provides "concrete evidence" of dangerousness. Id., at 364. By contrast, "[t]he only certain thing that can be said about the present state of knowledge and therapy regarding mental disease is that science has not reached finality of judgment. . . ." Id., at 365, n. 13 (quoting Greenwood v. United States, 350 U.S. 366, 375 (1956)). Given this uncertainty, "courts should pay particular deference to reasonable legislative judgments" about the relationship between dangerous behavior and mental illness. Jones, supra, at 365, n. 3. … we have consistently emphasized that "the Court has no license to invalidate legislation which it thinks merely arbitrary or unreasonable.""

[85] Kansas v. Hendricks, 521 U.S. 346 (1997)

"Contrary to Hendricks' argument, this Court has never required States to adopt any particular nomenclature in drafting civil commitment statutes and leaves to the States the task of defining terms of a medical nature that have legal significance. Cf. *Jones* v. *United States,* 463 U. S. 354, 365, n. 13. … In fact, it is precisely where such disagreement exists that legislatures have been afforded the widest latitude in drafting such statutes. Cf. *Jones* v. *United States, 463* U. S. 354, 365, n. 13 (1983). As we have explained regarding congressional enactments, when a legislature "undertakes to act in areas fraught with medical and scientific uncertainties, legislative options must be especially broad and courts

Stalin = ratio of harmless committed to violent set free

59. What is the real meaning of saying that 2 errors in 3 for predicting future violent behavior is "not entirely unreliable"? Every Justice who looked would find massive violations of civil liberties in just the sheer statistical inaccuracies of clinical predictions of future violent behavior. Stalin allegedly said, "Better that ten innocent men suffer than one spy escape." What would a 2/3 error rate produce? Consider the following variables and analysis:

C = the number of those evaluated who are committed as violent

R = the number of those evaluated released as non-violent

E = the number of people evaluated for commitment = $C + R$

Cr = commitment ratio = C/E, $0 \leq Cr \leq 1$ ➜ $C = Cr*E$, $R = (1-Cr)*E$

Tvc = true rate of violent people committed, $0 < Tvc < 1$

Tnr = true rate of non-violent people released, $0 < Tnr < 1$

Vc = the number of violent people committed = $C*Tvc$

Nc = the number of non-violent people committed = $C*(1-Tvc)$

Vr = the number of violent people released = $R*(1-Tnr)$

Nr = the number of non-violent people released = $R*Tnr$

Stalin = the ratio of non-violent people committed to violent people released

$$= (C*(1-Tvc))/(R*(1-Tnr)) = (Cr*(1-Tvc))/((1-Cr)*(1-Tnr))$$

---

should be cautious not to rewrite legislation." *Id.,* at 370 (internal quotation marks and citation omitted)."

60. Monahan (Circa 1981) [86] [87] [88] determined the value of Tvc to be about 1/3. Other research [89] [90] [91] has put the value of Tnr at 0.85 to 0.95. For the moment let Tnr = 0.90. More recent research[92] [93] [94] [95] [96] suggests that Tvc for clinical prediction of violent behavior may have improved to even chance or just above. Let this be represented by Tvc = 0.56. Then Table 1 and Figure 1 show the non-linear relationship between "Stalin", the ratio of harmless committed to violent released,

[86] Monahan, J. (1981). *The clinical prediction of violent behavior.* Washington, DC:Government Printing Office; Rockville, MD: National Institute of Mental Health, 1981. Science Library call no: WM 600 M734c 1981

[87] Monahan, John, 1995. The Clinical Prediction of Violent Behavior, 1995 softcover ed., Jason Aronson, Inc., Northvale, NJ & London, 134 p., over 200 references

[88] Barefoot v. Estelle, 463 U.S. 880 (1983)

[89] Monahan, John, 1995. The Clinical Prediction of Violent Behavior, 1995 softcover ed., Jason Aronson, Inc., Northvale, NJ & London, p 45, p 48.

[90] Scurich, NI, 2009, The effects of framing and actuarial risk probabilities on involuntary civil commitment decisions, a thesis presented to the faculty of the graduate school, University of Southern California, in partial fulfillment of the requirements for the Degree Master of Arts (Psychology)

[91] Fazel et al., 2012, Use of risk assessment instruments to predict violence and antisocial behavior in 73 samples involving 24,827 people: systematic review and meta-analysis, British Medical Journal, 2012;345:e4692.

[92] Scherr, Alexander, 2003, Daubert & Danger: The "Fit" of Expert Predictions in Civil Commitments, 55 HASTINGS L.J. 1, 2, 17–18 (2003).

[93] MacArthur Violence Risk Assessment Study, August 1996 Executive Summary, American Psychology-Law Society, Division 41, American Psychological Association, Fall 1996 Vol. 16, No. 3

[94] Beecher-Monas, Erica, 2003, The Epistemology of Prediction: Future Dangerousness Testimony and Intellectual Due Process, Washington and Lee Law Review, Volume 60 | Issue 2, 3-1-2003

[95] Krauss, DA, et al., 2004, The Effects of Rational and Experiential Information Processing of Expert Testimony in Death Penalty Cases, Behav. Sci. Law 22: 801–822 (2004)

and the commitment ratio, "Cr", the ratio of those committed to those evaluated. They clearly show that between commitment rates of 10% and 20%, both values of Tvc produce a ratio of one harmless person committed for every violent person released. Consider that psychiatric evaluators are largely shielded by law in the "good faith performance of their duties", which allows them to commit harmless people, but can be sued for damages if they release a violent person who then commits a murder or vicious assault. Note that for Cr = 60% and Tvc = 1/3, the ratio of harmless committed to violent released echoes Stalin's alleged comment. For Tvc = 0.56 and Cr = 0.693, Stalin = 10. Note that the logarithmic "Stalin" axis in Figure 1 denotes an exponential rise for a straight line on the graph.

Tvc =	0.333	0.560
Tnr =	0.900	0.900
Cr	Stalin-1	Stalin-2
0.01	0.067	0.044
0.10	0.741	0.489
0.20	1.667	1.100
0.30	2.857	1.886
0.40	4.444	2.933
0.50	6.667	4.400
0.60	10.000	6.600
0.70	15.556	10.267
0.80	26.667	17.600
0.90	60.000	39.600
0.99	660.000	435.600

Table 1: Stalin vs. Commitment Ratio for Tvc = 1/3 and 0.56

---

[96] Monahan, John, 6-1-2000, Violence Risk Assessment: Scientific Validity and Evidentiary Admissibility, Washington and Lee Law Rev, Article 8, 57(3):901-918

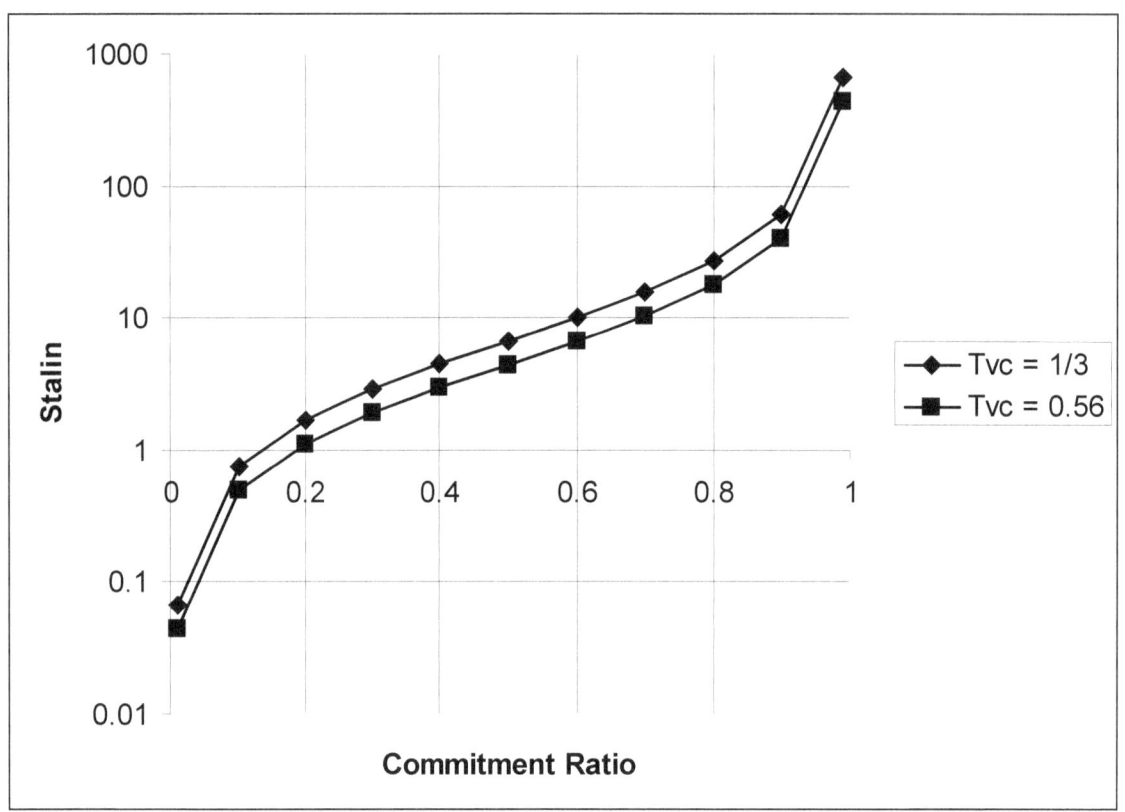

Figure 1: Stalin vs. Commitment Ratio for Tvc = 1/3 and 0.56

61. It seems unlikely that even a Justice of the Supreme Court of the United States would

appreciate an exponentially rising chance of being personally and falsely committed.

The consequences of Buck and Barefoot

The vast expansion of psychiatric legal power

62. Not only did Buck help spawn the huge expansion of eugenic sterilizations at home

and abroad, Buck and Barefoot provided psychiatry with legal powers of confinement

and coercion far beyond any other medical discipline. No other medical doctor can

force any patient to accept treatment just because the doctor thinks the patient needs it. For example, there is no Supreme Court decision upholding the right of any doctor or hospital to force a patient to accept plastic surgery merely because the patient is ugly in the doctor's opinion. People with missing limbs cannot be forced to use prosthetics. With the exception of some immunizations or quarantines in times of disease outbreaks, no one can be forced to accept non-psychiatric medical treatment, not even on pain of death. In every other medical discipline, treatment is voluntary under the principle of, "First, do no harm."

63. Not everyone got the memo. Psychiatry; and psychiatrists, like Medicare frauds, have often taken full advantage of that extra power. Buck (1927) established modern civil commitment proceedings, especially for vulnerable people without the financial resources to hire their own lawyers and expert witnesses: no counsel during psychiatric examinations; all the "expert witnesses" on the other side; lawyers for the patient either public defenders trained not to raise objections, or picked by the other side; hearsay accepted as proof; the medical "opinions" of psychiatric examiners taken as proof, valid or not; psychiatric examiners biased towards commitment.

64. Barefoot (1983) made sure that psychiatric examinations need not meet the exacting standards of other expert witnesses, as later defined by Daubert (1993)[97]. It is fair to

---

[97] Daubert v. Merrell Dow Pharmaceuticals, Inc., 509 U.S. 579 (1993)

"Standard used by a trial judge to make a preliminary assessment of whether an expert's scientific testimony is based on reasoning or methodology that is scientifically valid and can properly be applied to the facts at issue. Under this standard, the factors that may be considered in determining whether the methodology is valid are: (1) whether the theory or technique in question can be and has been tested; (2) whether it has been subjected to peer review and publication; (3) its known or potential error rate; (4) the existence and maintenance of standards controlling its operation; and (5) whether it has attracted

say that any other "expert witness" appearing in a court with a 2 in 3 error rate, or even not much better than flipping a coin, might well be laughed out of it. But this Court has never fully reconsidered civil commitments, or even involuntary eugenic sterilization, in the light of Daubert, leaving the public subject to the resulting and gaping moral hazards.

65. None of this happened in a vacuum[98]. In the 1950s and '60s, many State mental hospitals were exposed as snake pits, where the massive use of drugs took the place of actual treatment[99]. Releasing mental patients to community mental health facilities was oversold, as the money was never allocated to support them during the reduction

---

widespread acceptance within a relevant scientific community. See Daubert v. Merrell Dow Pharmaceuticals, Inc., 509 U.S. 579 (1993). The Daubert standard is the test currently used in the federal courts and some state courts. In the federal courts, it replaced the Frye standard."
[http://www.law.cornell.edu/wex/daubert_standard]

[98] McGuan, Elizabeth A. (2009) "New Standards for the Involuntary Commitment of the Mentally Ill: "Danger" Redefined," *Marquette Elder's Advisor: Vol. 11: Iss. 1, Article 10.* Available at: http://scholarship.law.marquette.edu/elders/vol11/iss1/10.

"In 1965, when the federal government enacted the Grants to States for Medical Assistance Program, known as Medicaid, which was "designed to improve healthcare for the poor by providing matching funds for state expenditures," it excluded psychiatric care provided in state-funded psychiatric hospitals." This exclusion created a major incentive for states to reduce the number of institutionalized patients and to close psychiatric hospitals altogether.[45]

"Regardless of the reasons, state and federal governments moved from a hospital-based setting to a community-based setting for the delivery of mental health services.[46] The governments failed, however, to provide funding to the community to support the increased population of mentally ill persons who received care there.[47] Because of the limited availability of medical care in the community,[48] the 1970s and 1980s became periods of "transinstitutionalization," as the mentally ill moved from hospitals to jails,[49] or to "open air" asylums" - the streets.[50]"

[99] Lyons, RD, 1984, How Release of Mental Patient Began, New York Times, Oct 30, 1984, http://www.nytimes.com/1984/10/30/science/how-release-of-me...

of the welfare state under President Reagan in the 1980s[100]. As with the Germans

during the economic collapse after WWI[101], attitudes hardened. Former mental

patients became the new homeless, and get tough on crime approaches put many of

them in prison, the new substitute mental health facilities[102 103 104 105 106]. As in

Germany, mental illness became closely associated with dangerous criminality,

continuing to this day. Let one disturbed person engage in a mass shooting and all

are suspect.

---

[100] Thomas, Alexandar, Ronald Reagan and the Commitment of the Mentally Ill: Capital, Interest Groups, and the Eclipse of Social Policy, Electronic Journal of Sociology (1998), http://sociology.org/content/vol003.004/thomas_d.html

[101] Mostert, Mark P., 2002, Useless Eaters: Disability as Genocidal Marker in Nazi Germany, 2002, http://www.catholicculture.org/culture/library/view.cfm?id=7019&repos=1&subrepos=0&searchid=11461 40 © 2013 Trinity Communications

[102] Torrey, EF, 1995, Jails and prisons - America's new mental hospitals. *Am J Public Health*, 85, 1611-1613

[103] Harlow, K, 2007, Applying the Reasonable Person Standard to Psychosis: How Tort Law Unfairly Burdens Adults with Mental Illness, Ohio State Law Journal, 68:1733-60

[104] Perlin, Micheal L., 1991, Competency, Deinstitutionalization, And Homelessness: A Story Of Marginalization, 28 Hous. L. Rev. 63

[105] Torrey, EF, 1997, Out of the Shadows: Confronting America's Mental Illness Crisis, New York: John Wiley & Sons,

"A second approach to assessing the relationship between deinstitutionalization and the increasing number of mentally ill people in jail prisons is to examine the reasons for incarceration. In the 1992 Public Citizen survey, investigators found that *29 percent* of the jails sometimes incarcerate persons *who have no charges against them* but are merely waiting for psychiatric evaluation, the availability of a psychiatric hospital bed, or transportation to a psychiatric hospital. Such jailings are done under state laws permitting emergency detentions of individuals suspected of being mentally ill and are especially common in rural states such as Kentucky, Mississippi, Alaska, Montana, Wyoming, and New Mexico."

Psychiatric hospital insurance scams

66. Around the time of Barefoot, the for-profit private psychiatric hospital industry began a large expansion, and needed to fill beds. Buck and Barefoot, giving the absolute credence of fact to mere medical opinion, provided the perfect legal cover. Following the Federal Trade Commission's 1982 decision under Pres. Reagan to lift the ban on medical advertising[107], psychiatric hospitals began advertising for parent to commit their own children for failing to meet academic or social standards, increasing the number of juveniles admitted by three times between 1980 and 1984[108]. Propelled in

---

[106] Loo, Hon. Cynthia, 2007, Predicting Violence in the Mentally Ill, The Criminal Docket, Criminal Justice Section of the Los Angeles County Bar Association, July 2007, Volume II, Number 2

[107] Mohr, Wanda K., 1998, Experiences of patients hospitalized during the Texas mental health scandal, Perspectives in Psychiatric Care, Vol 34, 1998

also: "The events surrounding the for-profit psychiatric hospital scandal occurred during a time described by Phillips (1990) as "a glorification of capitalism, free markets, and finance" (p. xvii). Wall Street firms expanded in a newly deregulated environment, and the focus of collective corporate management narrowed to an intense profit orientation. Company and executive incentives and bonuses were based on the profit margins they generated, and the frenetic pace of financial activity was reflected in the short-term perspective adopted by top executive offices. Quarterly earnings replaced long-term strategic planning as a focus of scrutiny. Together with a nonstop pressure to produce, "too often ... little attention [was paid] to methods employed" (Johnson, 1992, p. 237)."

[108] Boodman, Sandra, 1992, Ads for Psychiatric Hosptials Come Under Attack, The Washington Post, May 08, 1992,

"Between 1980 and 1986, admissions of juveniles to private psychiatric hospitals nearly tripled, rising from 17,000 to 43,000, according to the National Institute of Mental Health. Critics say this rapid expansion of inpatient psychiatric care for children and adolescents was fueled by parental insecurities, the elasticity of psychiatric diagnoses, the willingness of insurance companies to pay for hospitalization and relentless marketing by the hospitals themselves."

part by the expansion of definitions of mental illness in the Diagnostic and Statistical Manual of Mental Disorders (DSM) from 60 in 1957 to more than 200 in 1987[109].

67. Providing some of the most in-depth coverage of the psychiatric hospital insurance scandals, the Houston Chronicle's "Profitable Addictions" series, by staff writer Mark Smith and others, produced at least 42 articles covering those scandals in Texas, from about May 1989 to about March 1997. The scandals included not just false advertising and insurance scams, but torture[110], bounty hunters paid by hospitals to kidnap innocent and harmless people in off the streets[111], targeting the relatively rich benefits of military families[112], and committing children below the age of five[113].

---

[109] Mohr, 1998

[110] Smith, Mark, 1997, "Few doctors lost licenses over scandal/Psychiatric hospitals accused of filling beds `at any cost'", Houston Chronicle, MON 03/24/1997 HOUSTON CHRONICLE, Section A, Page 1, 3 STAR Edition,

"Flashbacks of the taunting and torture in the now-defunct Psychiatric Institute of Fort Worth continue to haunt Jeannie Warren.

"It's been nearly eight years since Warren's adoptive mother committed her to the for-profit psychiatric hospital. But Warren vividly recalls the terror of some two dozen "rage reduction" therapy sessions in which health workers pinned her down on a gym mat, then muffled her nose and mouth as her psychiatrist ground his fists into her ribs and stomach.

"The psychiatrist, Dr. Robert Hadley Gross, told Warren his actions were part of therapy designed to allow her to release underlying anger against her biological mother.

"I cried and hyperventilated," Warren recalled. "I stopped breathing twice. When I started breathing again they would slam me back down on the mat.""

[111] Smith, Mark, 1991, PROFITABLE ADDICTIONS/Captured and held against will/Some private hospitals prey on patients with insurance, Houston Chronicle 09/09/1991

"SAN ANTONIO - For Marianne Harrell, April 12 was a flashback to her childhood in Nazi Germany. Two huge men came to take her 14-year-old grandson away. They were private security company employees, and their mission was to deliver the youth to a corporate psychiatric hospital. The teen-ager

-27-

had not been physically evaluated by a doctor. Instead, the decision to come for him was made based on comments from his 12-year-old brother to a psychiatrist. ... She now never leaves her doors unlocked - even when she is home. She cringes whenever she sees a patrol car."

[112] Smith, Mark, 1992, Profitable Addictions/Abuses in mental health programs are pinpointed, Houston Chronicle. 04/29/1992, Section A, p 1,2,

"WASHINGTON -- One-third of the more than $600 million in mental health claims filed by military employees and their dependents in fiscal 1990 were "medically unnecessary," a General Accounting Office study indicates.The GAO report, released Tuesday during a congressional hearing on abuses in the private psychiatric hospital industry, also found nearly two-thirds of the mental health claims filed to the Civilian Health and Medical Plan for the Uniformed Services, or CHAMPUS, were for treatment considered medically questionable. ... Texas led the nation with the greatest number of these claims, $132 million in fiscal 1990 or bout a fifth of all claims."

[113] Smith, Mark, & Cindy Rugeley, 1993, State probes psychiatric care of youth Morales checks into legality of expensive hospitalizations, SUN 11/21/1993 HOUSTON CHRONICLE, Section A, Page 1, 2 STAR Edition,

"A Department of Human Services sampling of claims during a three-month period earlier this year showed 35 percent of the cases didn't qualify for all of the state payments they received, either because the child should not have been admitted at all or because the child stayed in the hospital longer than necessary. It also found nearly half of the children admitted during the period were diagnosed as suffering from "major depression disorder," with the second-highest number being admitted for "disturbance of conduct," such as running away from home, truancy from school, breaking into a home or using a weapon in a fight. Health Department records show that in the most recent fiscal year, the early screening program paid for 3,339 people under age 21 to be treated in private psychiatric hospitals. That included 205 children from ages 1 to 5. An additional 2,272 children ages 6 to 14 were admitted to the hospitals under the program. ... "I can think of almost no circumstances where a 2-year-old should be in a psychiatric hospital. That's been a problem and I think the state recognizes that," said Dr. Mike McKinney, a former state representative who is now medical director of National Heritage Insurance Co., which contracts with the state to administer Medicaid payments."

68. Other reports demonstrated widespread abuse across the nation [114] [115] [116] [117] [118] [119] [120].

[114] Sileo, Chi Chi, 1994, Rip-off depress mental health care – fraud in psychiatric hospital practices, Insight on the News, Jan 24, 1994,

"In 1992, hearings held by the House Select Committee on Children, Youth and Families revealed even more desperate measures by hospitals -- some going beyond advertising to outright kidnapping. According to testimony at the hearings, chaired by Colorado Democrat Patricia Schroeder, some hospitals were hiring private security guards to pick people up and keep them hospitalized against their will. Kyle Williams of San Antonio, Texas, testified that he was picked up from his workplace by two men in badges whom he mistook for police officers. He was locked in a psychiatric hospital for days, he said, given tranquilizers and pressured to sign commitment papers. He was released only when his lawyer obtained a court order."

[115] Stevens, Lawrence, J.D. circa 2000, Unjustified Psychiatric Commitment in the U.S.A., www.antipsychiatry.org.

"In 1992, U.S. Representative Patricia Schroeder of Colorado held hearings investigating the practices of psychiatric hospitals in the United States. Rep. Schroeder summarized her committee's findings as follows: "Our investigation has found that thousands of adolescents, children, and adults have been hospitalized for psychiatric treatment they didn't need; that hospitals hire bounty hunters to kidnap patients with mental health insurance; that patients are kept against their will until their insurance benefits run out; that psychiatrists are being pressured by the hospitals to increase profit; that hospitals 'infiltrate' schools by paying kickbacks to school counselors who deliver students; that bonuses are paid to hospital employees, including psychiatrists, for keeping the hospital beds filled; and that military dependents are being targeted for their generous mental health benefits. I could go on, but you get the picture" (quoted in: Lynn Payer, *Disease- Mongers: How Doctors, Drug Companies, and Insurers Are Making You Feel Sick*, John Wiley & Sons, Inc., 1992, pp. 234-235)."

[116] Kerr, Peter, 1992, Government review finds 64% of psychiatric hospital stays aren't needed, New York Times News Service April 29, 1992

[117] Deneen, Sally, 1988, Complaints about psychiatric hospitals rise, August 19, 1988, Sun-Sentinel, Florida

[118] Rappaport, Richard G., MD, 2006, Losing Your Rights: Complications of Misdiagnosis, J Am Acad Psychiatry Law 34:4:436-438 (December 2006),

"Violation of civil rights, forced treatment, and commitment under the guise of psychiatric care occurred in two cases involving women who became "patients" in nonmedical situations in different

Some reports have noted the refusal of attorneys appointed for people with mental illness under threat of commitment to represent them with any vigor[121] [122], including

---

states. They were both violently victimized and at some point in their cases acted on their own behalf. One case will be described herein."

[119] Nadler, Art, 1998, Several claim they've been hospitalized against their will, Las Vegas Sun, Jan 24, 1998,

"Under a state law called a Legal 97, anyone in Nevada exhibiting signs of mental illness can be picked up and held against his will in a mental institution. … One case cited by Moore involves a man who was involuntarily committed last fall to Charter Behavioral Health System of Nevada after he was brought to University Medical Center. A Charter nurse recommended that the man be admitted, citing, among other things, that the man threatened his sister, Moore said. But his sister denies that her brother threatened her. …

"Nancy Patnaude was another former patient of Charter Hospital who says she was held against her will under a Legal 97. … Patnaude said the receptionist at Charter asked a few questions, then left and returned a few minutes later with a woman who identified herself as a nurse. Patnaude recounted how she felt the night before and that she was shopping around for counseling. The nurse, she alleges, recommended Charter's 21-day, in-house stay. "I said I wasn't interested in that, and that I needed to work and was interested in counseling on an out-patient basis," Patnaude said. "I didn't want to be rude, so I said she could show me their facility, and that I would keep them in mind." When the woman finished with the tour, Patnaude remembers her suddenly stepping back and saying she was sorry but that "it's out of my control." "At first I didn't know what she meant, and then I noticed exactly where I was standing," Patnaude said. "I was in a hall with her at one end, and two men in white coats, just like on television, standing behind me. "I said, 'You mean I can't leave?' She said, 'That's right.' I was never so frightened in my life. The two men came over and told me I could either go quietly, or they would strap me down. I went quietly.""

[120] Electric Shocks Are Inhumane And Barbaric, http://www.cchrflorida.org/blog/electric-shocks-areinhumane-and-barbaric/ and http://www.youtube.com/watch?v=RlJ10qnrfl4& (more recent abuse of a young boy at a mental facility named after a Judge)

[121] Gottstein, James B., 2008, Involuntary commitment and forced psychiatric drugging in the trial courts: rights violations as a matter of course, Alaska Law Review, Vol. 25:51-105

[122] Perlin, Michael L., 1994, *The ADA and Persons with Mental Disabilities: Can Sanist Attitudes Be Undone?* by Journal of Law and Health, 1993/1994, 8 JLHEALTH 15, 27p,

the willingness for "expert witnesses" to perjure themselves about the "dangerousness" of the patient, to obtain commitments for alleged good of the patient[123] [124] [125]. Considering the Buck, Addington and Barefoot principles that

---

[123] Gottstein, JB, 2002, Psychiatry: Force of Law, Nov 2002, PsychRights, Law Project for Psychiatric Rights, psychrights.org, citing Torrey, E.F, 1997, *Out of the Shadows: Confronting America's Mental Illness Crisis*. New York: John Wiley and Sons,

"It would probably be difficult to find any American Psychiatrist working with the mentally ill who has not, at a minimum, exaggerated the dangerousness of a mentally ill person's behavior to obtain a judicial order for commitment."

[124] Olberg, Becky, 2011, The Abuse of Psychiatric Detention and Its Complications, http://www.healthyplace.com/blogs/borderline/2011/02/the-abu..., citing the false use of immediate or emergency detention to serve non-psychiatric agendas, such as quarantine for pinkeye, and

"This happened to me once. I've forgotten what led up to it, but there was a heated argument with a therapist. The psychiatrist on call, without speaking to me, ordered an emergency evaluation. After I sat in the crisis intervention unit for several hours, a social worker came to evaluate me. She examined my arms and seemed surprised to see no fresh wounds. "[Therapist] said in your ID that you pulled out a knife and started cutting on yourself," she explained." …

"In 2009, I became severely ill with bronchitis. While my symptoms were not severe enough to warrant hospitalization, my doctor could not see me for a month. As the illness became worse, my psychiatrist realized I needed prompt medical attention. She IDed me so I would receive that treatment. Although understandable–and I'm grateful she did so before it went into pneumonia–it is still problematic. An ID is a difficult thing to deal with–especially the part involving the police handcuffs. An ID can save lives. It can also derail them."

[125] Perlin, Michael L., 1993/1994, The ADA and Persons with Mental Disabilities: Can Sanist Attitudes Be Undone?, Journal of Law and Health, 1993/1994 Symposium, 8 JLHEALTH 15, 27p,

"The entire relationship between the legal process and litigants with mental disabilities is often pretextual. By this I mean simply that courts accept (either implicitly or explicitly) testimonial dishonesty, and engage similarly in dishonest (frequently meretricious) decision making, specifically where witnesses, especially *expert* witnesses, show a "high propensity to purposely distort their testimony in order to achieve desired ends." [FN95] This pretextuality is poisonous. Its toxin infects all participants in the judicial system, breeds cynicism and disrespect for the law, demeans participants,

psychiatrists and other "licensed mental health professionals"[126] can tell only truth and do only good, they generally faced (and face) little or no consequences for falsifying commitments[127], so long as they maintain the appearance of justice and procedural protections. Besides which, in a recent December 2015 decision, this Court refused to hear an appeal from the 7th Circuit in the case of Friedman v. Highland Park, opining that even if the Constitutional rights of some group were infringed, any false sense of security the infringement imparts to the public could justify it. So it was with Dred Scott, Buck v. Bell, Addington and Barefoot. Therefore, it seems unlikely that this Court would break its own stare decisis with the Holocaust merely to bring justice to a despised minority, at the risk of displeasing a majority full of fear and loathing.

---

and reinforces shoddy lawyering, blase judging, and, at times, perjurious and/or corrupt testifying. The reality is well known to frequent consumers of judicial services in this area" …

"[FN33]. See Michael L. Perlin, Pretexts and Mental Disability Law: The Case of Competency, 47 U. MIAMI L. REV. 625 (1992) [hereinafter Perlin, *Pretexts*]; Michael L. Perlin, *Morality & Pretextuality, Psychiatry and Law: Of "Ordinary Common Sense," Heuristic Reasoning, and Cognitive Dissonance,* 19 BULL. AM. ACAD. PSYCHIATRY & L. 131 (1991) [hereinafter Perlin, *Morality*]."

"[FN95]. Perlin, Morality, supra note 33, at 133; e.g., Charles M. Sevilla, The Exclusionary Rule and Police Perjury, 11 SAN DIEGO L. REV. 839, 840 (1974)."

[126] Oklahoma State Code, Title 43A-1-103.11 in "Definitions"

[127] Smith, Mark, 1997, "Few doctors lost licenses over scandal/Psychiatric hospitals accused of filling beds `at any cost'", Houston Chronicle, MON 03/24/1997 HOUSTON CHRONICLE, Section A, Page 1, 3 STAR Edition,

"The action against Warren's therapist, however, is unusual. He was one of only five doctors and six others in Texas who faced criminal charges following a scandal that swept for-profit psychiatric hospitals in the late 1980s and early 1990s. Six hospital officials and two psychologists were charged in other states."

The workplace violence consulting industry

69. Three years after Barefoot, a postal worker named Patrick Sherrill killed 14 co-workers in Edmond, Oklahoma[128]. Due in part to a U.S. Post Office management model which demanded abusing subordinates to induce productivity[129], it spawned a number of copy-cat mass killings, and a huge public media response, with the code-words for violent mentally illness, "going postal". This in turn spawned a consulting industry, founded much less on science than advertising, promising quick fixes to alert employers to "dangers of violence in the workplace". While the primary cause of death and injury in the workplace remained workplace physical conditions, and the vast majority of people with mental illness were non-violent, the new model of violence prevention targeted anyone with a mental illness.

70. Almost as soon as the EEOC Employment Guidance on Psychiatric Disabilities was published, businesses fought back and editorials appeared with cartoons about the EEOC forcing employers to hire axe murderers and crazy Napoleons[130]. It became so rabid that in 1998 merely having nightmares about being a victim in a workplace mass shooting became a firing offense[131]. Up into at least 2001, the U.S. Department

---

[128] Laden, Vicki A. and Gregory Schwartz, 2000 Psychiatric Disabilities, the Americans with Disabilities Act, and the New Workplace Violence Account, *BERKELEY JOURNAL OF EMPLOYMENT & LABOR LAW* [Vol. 21:246-270, 2000

[129] Personal recollection of news magazine article

[130] USCCR, 2000, "Sharing the Dream: Is the ADA Accommodating All?", U.S. Commission on Civil Rights, Oct 2000, Chapter 5, Psychiatric Disabilities and the ADA, Usccr.gov-pubs-ada-ch5.htm – web page, www.usccr.gov/pubs/ada/main.htm

[131] Laden & Schwartz, 2000, p 248

of Agriculture put out training modules identifying anyone with a mental illness as being "a potential of violence in the workplace", which made any single loss of temper a firing offense[132]. Perhaps because few of these terminations for "dangerous" mental illness will show in public records, it may be that no one will ever know how many thousands or tens of thousands have been terminated out of mere fear and loathing.

The judicial gutting of the Americans with Disabilities Act

71. About the same time, this Court (and others) rendered decisions[133] on the 1990 Americans with Disabilities Act that sharply curtailed the employability of anyone with a disability, especially those with psychiatric disabilities[134] [135]. This Court shifted the emphasis of the ADA, from an employer proving an adequate attempt to accommodate an employee's disability, to what an employer should not have to put up with in the employee. Considering that, and the Barefoot principle that anyone who claims "100% accuracy" in predicting violence cannot be discounted because there is no "convincing evidence that it is almost entirely unreliable" (any smidgen of accuracy will do), it seems unlikely that the postal worker fired merely for having

---

[132] Personal experience

[133] Sutton v. United Airlines, 527 U.S. 471 (1999); Murphy v.United Parcel Service, 527 U.S. 516 (1999); Albertson's v. Kirkingburg, 527 U.S. 555 (1999); and Toyota v. Williams, 534 U.S. 184 (2002)

[134] National Council on Disability, 2003, The Americans with Disabilities Act Policy Brief Series: No. 7 The Impact of the Supreme Court's ADA Decisions on the Rights of Persons With Disabilities, February 25, 2003, http://www.ncd.gov/newsroom/publications/2003/decisionsimpact.htm

[135] USCCR, 2000, "Sharing the Dream: Is the ADA Accommodating All?"

nightmares about being a victim of a mass shooting could have his or her job reinstated before this Court.

72. In Toyota v. Williams, 534 U.S. 184 (2002), this Court went to extreme lengths to deny jobs she could do to a woman with severe carpal tunnel syndrome, who could not work at length without damage with her arms above her shoulders. Employing the Japanese cultural principle that everyone must work hard to do all the same things equally[136], Toyota required that all employees must be able to work in all positions on the factory floor. Williams tried to accommodate Toyota when it moved her to an assembly position that severely aggravated her condition. Informed by her doctor that she had to rest or suffer severe damage, she took time off and was fired. Noting that Williams could work in her garden and play with her children, this Court Decided that she did not have a disabling condition covered by the ADA. Thus this Court effectively found that productive employment was not a "major life activity" in order to accommodate Toyota's imported business culture.

73. When this Court can turn people with valid physical disabilities into second-class citizens who have no right to work, it must surely regard people with mental illnesses as third-class citizens who have no right to speak. One can see this clearly in such State mental health codes as Oklahoma's Title 43A. In the Definitions section, OSC-43A-1-103, a "Person requiring treatment" includes anyone with a mental illness

---

[136] Spiegel, Alix, 2012, Struggle For Smarts? How Eastern And Western Cultures Tackle Learning, NPR Morning Edition, November 12, 2012 4:00 AM,
http://www.npr.org/blogs/health/2012/11/12/164793058/struggle...

deemed a danger to him or her self or others. And "Risk of harm to self or others" includes:

> c. having placed another person or persons in a
> reasonable fear of violent behavior directed
> towards such person or persons or serious
> physical harm to them as manifested by serious and immediate threats,

74. Every bigot is reasonable, just ask the Buck and Dred Scott Courts.

Disparities in rights

75. In 2009 and 2010, a white supremacist group calling itself the Hutaree Militia held meetings in which it discussed killing police and then bombing the resulting funeral processions. The U.S. Government charged members with: (1) Seditious Conspiracy (18 U.S.C. § 2384); (2) Conspiracy to use Weapons of Mass Destruction (18 U.S.C. § 2332a(a)(2)); (3) Use and Carrying of a Firearm During and in Relation to a Crime of Violence (18 U.S.C. § 924(c)(1)); and (4) Possessing a Firearm in Furtherance of a Crime of Violence (18 U.S.C. § 924(c)(1)). In addition, Defendants David Stone, David Stone, Jr., and Joshua Stone are charged with weapons-related offenses.

76. In 2012, the case was dismissed in the U.S. District Court for the Eastern District of Michigan, Southern Division[137]. According to the trial judge, the Hon. Victoria A. Roberts, the Government had to show that there was a specific plan to violate the law, that each conspirator "possessed the knowledge and intent to join the conspiracy", and that each defendant participated in the conspiracy. Among other things, she held that 1) the plots involved could not be sedition because an attack on a local law

---

[137] U.S.A v. Stone, et al., Fed. Dist. Ct. MIED, 2:10-cr-20123-VAR-PJK, (3/27/2012)

enforcement authority was not an attack on the U.S. Government, 2) conspiracy with a government informer is not a true conspiracy, since there was no plan hatched between David Stone, Sr., and the other Defendants, 3) that while disturbing and offensive, Stone's remarks consisted mostly of ranting about his hateful desires to cause war, death and destruction, 4) there was no agreement on specific actions against the Federal Government, 5) attending firearms training sessions and making offensive remarks does not rise to conspiracy, and 6) the other charges being dependent upon the conspiracy charges, they are all dismissed.

77. So in other words, a person or pack of nutty, hateful, armed white supremacists can talk all they want to about doing violence to people they don't like, and it's just freedom of speech[138], so long as they don't agree on any specific plan of action and demonstrate intent to carry it out. But if one person taking medication for depression or PTSD talks about legitimate and lethal self-defense, after having an officer of the law explain the limits of it in a group setting, then if anyone, even a bully, even falsely, claims to have a "reasonable fear of violent behavior"[139], that person with a mental illness may be handcuffed in front of his or her neighbors by police, dragged off to the local loony bin, and incarcerated and drugged until proving the negative, that he or she is not a threat.

78. By upholding this disparity, this Court demonstrates the same kind of unequal treatment under the law that the Scott Court (1856) did towards negro slaves, the

---

[138] Amendment 1

[139] OSC 43A-1-103.18.c

Gould Court (1905) did towards epileptics, and the Buck Court (1927) did towards "feeble-minded" poor and colored people, by holding that it is "equally applied" to the group of all people with mental illness, no matter how distorted by enduring eugenic bigotry.

A salutary effect

79. So it would have a salutary effect on each Mister and Madam Justice of the Supreme Court of the United States if each and every one were dressed in dirt and old clothes, and left, suffering from heat exhaustion, and falsely accused of threatening behavior sufficient to warrant examination at the local loony bin, in separate places where no one knows his or her name or office or face. In such circumstances, claims of being a Justice of the Supreme Court would be taken as delusional, and excuse for involuntary civil commitment. Then, if each and every Justice were to explode in outrage, each and every Justice would get a shot of psychoactive drug to calm him or her down. Followed by weeks or months of confinement to an intellectual desert with coloring book and rubber chicken therapy, where none could be released to outpatient parole until proving the negative to skeptical psychiatrists, that he or she is not a danger to self or society.

80. Depending on the individual susceptibility of each Justice to depression, and the number of times release had been promised, scheduled and withdrawn, one or more might consider suicide as a means of escape, and find ways that it might be accomplished either in a fraction of a second in front of medical tormentors, or in between bed checks at night. Then, after release, each susceptible Justice might well find that the after-effects of such "medical treatment" include shaking like a Chihuahua and crying at every

instance of heat stress or fatigue. Each such Justice might even decide that in the event of any future threat of commitment or arrest, he or she has no obligation to be taken alive, and if taken alive, to remain alive. Perhaps in part because he or she will find that productive employment in his or her old profession is no longer possible, if only because the load of additional medication will destroy the intellectual ability to do it, never mind the stigma.

81. Such an experience might provoke each and every Justice to examine the law, case law, alleged science and medicine, history and bigotry which made it possible. If so, each and every Justice would find his or her own Court at the center of the web.

REASONS FOR GRANTING THE PETITION

This Court cannot guarantee the souls of men

82. As a practical matter, this Court can set legal procedure, interpret law and guarantee the Constitution of the United States, but it cannot guarantee the souls of men. Where it has tried to describe and guarantee the good behavior of men, it erred and failed, creating gaping moral hazards, which evil men may exploit for their gain merely by acting the opposite. Despite its many opinions to the contrary involving mental health and eugenics, it cannot even guarantee the good behavior of medical doctors, as generations of the practitioners of Medicare fraud and abuse have demonstrated, and in such ventures as the Tuskegee Experiments.

Junk science and moral hazards

83. To justify lower standards of evidence and procedure for civil commitment, this Court has assumed more than once both that medical treatment cannot be punishment or be intended as punishment, and thus created moral and ethical hazards. In the presence of such hazards, at least some men will inevitably fail to pass the test, and cause horrific prejudice and injustice [140] [141] [142]. As the 1856 Scott and 1927 Buck Decisions have

---

[140] Mostert, Mark P., 2002, Useless Eaters: Disability as Genocidal Marker in Nazi Germany, 2002, http://www.catholicculture.org/culture/library/view.cfm?id=7019&repos=1&subrepos=0&searchid=11461 40 © 2013 Trinity Communications

"It is important to note that the enactment of prejudice against people with disabilities in Nazi Germany could not have succeeded without the complicity of the medical and adjunct professions. Power over life and death was placed firmly in the hands of physicians who became white-coated executioners, having long abandoned the "do no harm" clause of the Hippocratic Oath. Currently, there is evidence of the medical community's again being willing agents in hastening the deaths of people deemed not viable, including people with disabilities, through familiar methods for ending the lives of terminally ill people, such as starvation and death by thirst. Furthermore, there is evidence that "do no harm" is now viewed as a somewhat quaint throwback to a distant, less sophisticated era. For example, many physicians no longer take the Hippocratic Oath before beginning their careers, and many standard hospital treatment protocols now stipulate that staff physicians may override next-of-kin requests for patient treatment if the physician decides that treatment will likely be ineffective (Smith, 2000). Once again, patients, including those with disabilities who are terminally ill, now bear the responsibility of justifying their existence and their need for treatment. This being the case, and with the clear understanding that not all physicians put the greater good ahead of their individual patients, there should at least be some debate about what this means for people with disabilities, many of whom rely extensively on the assumption that their physicians have their best individual treatment interests at heart and will treat them regardless of utilitarian arguments to the contrary."

[141] History of Psychiatric Insitutions, 2013, Wikipedia, http://en.wikipedia.org/wiki/History_of_psychiatric_institutions,

"Under Nazi Germany, the Aktion T4 euthanasia program resulted in the killings of thousands of the mentally ill housed in state institutions. In 1939, the Nazis secretly began to exterminate the mentally ill in a euthanasia campaign. Around 6,000 disabled babies, children and teenagers were murdered by starvation or lethal injection.[32: Torrey E.F., Yolken R.H. (16 September 2009). "Psychiatric Genocide: Nazi Attempts to Eradicate Schizophrenia" (http://www.schizophreniaforum.org/images/livedisc /PsychiatricGenocide.pdf). Schizophrenia Bulletin 36 (1): 1–7. doi:10.1093/schbul/sbp097 (http://dx.doi.org /10.1093%2Fschbul%2Fsbp097). PMC 2800142 (//www.ncbi.nlm.nih.gov/pmc/articles/PMC2800142). PMID 19759092 (//www.ncbi.nlm.nih.gov/pubmcd/19759092).] " …

"Psychiatrists around the world have been involved in the suppression of individual rights by states wherein the definitions of mental disease had been expanded to include political disobedience.[35]:6 Nowadays, in many countries, political prisoners are sometimes confined to mental institutions and abused therein.[36]:3 Psychiatry possesses a built-in capacity for abuse which is greater than in other areas of medicine.[37]:65 The diagnosis of mental disease can serve as proxy for the designation of social dissidents, allowing the state to hold persons against their will and to insist upon therapies that work in favour of ideological conformity and in the broader interests of society.[37]:65 In a monolithic state, psychiatry can be used to bypass standard legal procedures for establishing guilt or innocence and allow political incarceration without the ordinary odium attaching to such political trials.[37]:65 In Nazi Germany in the 1940s, the 'duty to care' was violated on an enormous scale: A reported 300,000 individuals were sterilized and 100,000 killed in Germany alone, as were many thousands further afield,

amply demonstrated, from slavery to Jim Crow, to strange fruit hanging in Southern

trees, to the mass sterilization of poor and colored people without their knowledge or

consent, to the mass commitment of harmless and healthy people to satisfy psychiatric

hospital insurance scams, which even sent out bounty hunters to drag plausible

candidates in off the streets, down to the unjustifiable police harassment and shootings of

young black men in this day.

84.   Further, historians have shown how the Court of Oliver Wendell Holmes, through

the 1927 Buck v. Bell decision, based upon the junk science of eugenics, which this

Court has never seen fit to fully refute, bears a substantial measure of direct responsibility

for the Nazi Holocaust [143] [144] [145] [146] [147] [148] [149] [150] [151]. As a consequence, the very name

---

mainly in eastern Europe.[38] From the 1960s up to 1986, political abuse of psychiatry was reported to
be systematic in the Soviet Union, and to surface on occasion in other Eastern European countries such
as Romania, Hungary, Czechoslovakia, and Yugoslavia.[37]:66 A "mental health genocide" reminiscent
of the Nazi aberrations has been located in the history of South African oppression during the apartheid
era.[39] A continued misappropriation of the discipline was subsequently attributed to the People's
Republic of China.[40]"

[142] Alexander, George J., 1997, International Human Rights Protection Against Psychiatric Political
Abuses, 37 Santa Clara L. Rev. 387 (1997),

"The decision regarding which patients should be killed [in WWII German medical facilities] was made
entirely by expert consultants, most of whom were professors of psychiatry in key universities. These
consultants never saw the patients themselves. [see also Barefoot v. Estelle, 1983, for similar reasoning
and justification] ... In the beginning, it was useful to the Nazis to describe incarceration as cure and
care and killing as charity [not intended as punishment, as in Addington v. Texas, 1979 at Page 441 U.
S. 428]. Only later was broader genocide possible more openly. That utility has not escaped some
governments which also use coercive psychiatry to achieve political ends."

[143] Grodin, Michael and George Annas, 2007, Physicians and torture: lessons from the Nazi doctors, Int'l
Review of the Red Cross, Volume 89 Number 867 September 2007,

"The idea of racial hygiene emerged at the turn of the twentieth century, and the racial policies of the Third Reich were in many ways adapted from eugenics practices developed in the United States in the early twentieth century.[12] ...

"In the US Supreme Court decision Buck v. Bell, referring to the fact that the state can draft people into military service, the Court concluded, ... Three generations of imbeciles are enough.[14] Ultimately, the Nazis would carry this ideology beyond sterilization.

" By 1937, the representation of doctors in the SS – the most vicious arm of the Nazi Party – was seven times higher than that of the average for the employed male population and by 1942, 50 per cent of all German doctors had joined the Nazi Party.[20]"

[144] Kindregan, C.P., 1966, Sixty Years of Compulsory Eugenic Sterilization: Three Generations of Imbeciles and the Constitution of the United States, Chicago-Kent Law Review, Volume 43 | Issue 2, pp 123-43,

"At Nuremberg, American judges condemned the Nazi use of the German CES laws to eliminate "undesirable" characteristics from the race, but it was the American states which had "pioneered" the use of CES. The law is only as strong as the protection which it gives to its weakest subjects. Viewed by the standards of the Constitution of the United States, twenty-five states retain laws which are open to gross abuse of the rights of the most dependent and weakest citizens. ... Respect for Mr. Justice Holmes must not prevent the courts from admitting the fallacious absurdity of his reasoning in *Bell v. Buck.* Our science, our common sense, but most importantly our Constitution demand an end to CES in the United States."

[145] Rubin, Nilmini Gunaratne, 2012, A crime against motherhood - Involuntary sterilization was a horrifying exercise in genetic engineering, Los Angeles Times, May 13, 2012, http://articles.latimes.com/2012/may/13/opinion/la-oe-rubin-eugenics-mothers-day-20120513

"The word "eugenics" was coined in 1883 by a British scientist, Francis Galton, who was Charles Darwin's half-cousin. In the U.S. the movement was championed by wealthy elites like John Harvey Kellogg, doctor, corn flakes magnate and creator of the Race Betterment Foundation in Battle Creek, Mich. The Nazis relied on eugenics research financed by the Carnegie Institution and the Rockefeller Foundation. ... The U.S. Supreme Court upheld forced sterilization in 1927, a decision that still stands. Justice Oliver Wendell Holmes wrote in the majority decision, "It is better for all the world, if instead of waiting to execute degenerate offspring for crime, or to let them starve for their imbecility, society can prevent those who are manifestly unfit from continuing their kind.... Three generations of imbeciles are enough." At the Nuremberg trials, Nazis quoted Holmes in their defense."

[146] Buck v. Bell, 2013, from Wikipedia, http://en.wikipedia.org/wiki/Buck_v._Bell,

"The Virginia statute which the ruling of *Buck v. Bell* supported was designed in part by the eugenicist Harry H. Laughlin, superintendent of Charles Benedict Davenport's Eugenics Record Office in Cold Spring Harbor, New York. … Laughlin saw the need to create a "Model Law"[12] which could withstand a test of constitutional scrutiny, clearing the way for future sterilization operations. Adolf Hitler closely modelled his Law for the Prevention of Hereditarily Diseased Offspring on Laughlin's "Model Law". The Third Reich held Laughlin in such regard that they arranged for him to receive an honorary doctorate from Heidelberg University in 1936. At the Nuremberg trials after World War II, Nazi doctors explicitly cited Holmes's opinion in Buck v. Bell as part of their defense.[13]"

[147] Mehler, Barry, 1987, 'Eliminating the Inferior: American and Nazi Sterilization Programs,' Science for the People (Nov-Dec 1987) pp. 14-18,

"Whether the social and philosophical objectives of sterilization advocates diverged into democratic and totalitarian camps during the 1930s or not, with regard to eugenic sterilization, the United States served as an example to the rest of the world. The first sterilization law was passed in Indiana in 1907. From that year until 1928, when the first European sterilization law was passed in the Swiss Canton de Vaud, Americans had enacted nearly thirty state sterilization laws. Between 1928 and 1936, a number of European nations also passed sterilization laws, including Denmark (1929), Germany (1933), Sweden and Norway (1934), Finland and Danzig (1935), and Estonia (1936). All of these laws, according to Dr. Marie Kopp, who toured Germany studying the administration of Nazi Sterilization laws for the American Eugenics Society in 1935, were modeled and inspired by American efforts.(4)"

[148] Nilsson, Kevin, circa 2000, Eugenics: A Historical Analysis,
http://campus.udayton.edu/~hume/Eugenics/eugenics.htm

"In 1933 the Nazi party seized control of Germany and forever altered public opinion of eugenics. Initially, the Nazis enacted only sterilization laws. However, these laws went far beyond the actions of the United States. In *Mein Kampf* Hitler wrote that "anyone who wants to cure this era, which is inwardly sick and rotten, must first of all summon up the courage to make clear the causes of the disease." (David, 89) The Nazi party took several steps to rid the Third Reich of the "causes of the disease.""

[149] Skinner v. Oklahoma, 2013, Wikipedia, http://en.wikipedia.org/wiki/Skinner_v._Oklahoma,

"The only types of sterilization which the ruling immediately ended were punitive sterilizations—it did not directly comment on compulsory sterilization of the mentally disabled or mentally ill and was not a strict overturning of the Court's ruling in *Buck v. Bell* (1927). Furthermore, most of the over 64,000 sterilizations performed in the USA under the aegis of eugenics legislation were not in prison institutions or performed on convicted criminals; punitive sterilizations made up only negligible amounts of the total operations performed, as most states and prison officials were nervous about their legal status (which were not affirmed in *Buck v. Bell* specifically) as possible violations of the Eighth ("cruel and unusual punishment") or Fourteenth Amendments ("Due Process" and "Equal Protection Clauses"). Compulsory sterilizations of the mentally disabled and mentally ill continued in the USA in significant numbers until the early 1960s. Though many of their laws stayed on the books for many years longer, the last known forced sterilization in the United States occurred in 1981 in Oregon.[2] Over one-third of all compulsory sterilizations in the United States (over 22,670) took place after *Skinner v. Oklahoma.*

"The 1942 ruling did, however, create a nervous legal atmosphere regarding these other forms of sterilizations, and put a heavy damper on sterilization rates which had boomed since the *Buck v. Bell* ruling in 1927. After the discovery of the Nazi atrocities done in the name of eugenics—including the compulsory sterilization of 450,000 individuals in barely more than a decade under a sterilization law which drew heavy inspiration from American statutes—and the close association between eugenics and racism, eugenics as an ideology lost almost all public favor.

"In Equal Protection analysis, *Skinner* applied the compelling state interest test to punitive sterilization, whereas *Buck* applied the less rigorous rational basis test to compulsory sterilization of the mentally disabled."

150 Claude Moore Health Sciences Library, 2004, Influence | Eugenics: Three Generations, No Imbeciles: Virginia, Eugenics & Buck v. Bell, U. of Virginia, http://exhibits.hsl.virginia.edu/eugenics/4-influence/,

"The impact of the *Buck v. Bell* decision was felt nationwide. After the 1927 decision affirmed Virginia's Eugenical Sterilization Law, there was a swift rise in the number of involuntary sterilizations in the United States. By the early 1930s, thirty American states had adopted eugenics laws. American eugenicists also pushed for anti-immigration measures and stricter laws to prevent racially mixed marriages. When signing the 1924 Immigration Restriction Act, President Calvin Coolidge stated: "America must remain American."

"For a time, the doctrine of eugenics exerted considerable influence on American society. Based largely on political and social prejudices, the pseudoscience was taught at schools and universities. Leading institutions, such as Harvard, Cornell, Columbia, and the University of Virginia offered courses in eugenics. ... Using language from Laughlin's Model Law, Germany's Nazi government adopted the Law for Protection Against Genetically Defective Offspring in 1933 that provided the legal basis for sterilizations in Germany. In its first full year of operation, the Nazi program dramatically eclipsed activities in the United States, sterilizing about 80,000 persons without their consent. The much grander scope was achieved because the Nazi law applied to the entire population rather than just institutionalized persons. A system of hereditary health courts was designed exclusively to hear and

"Doctor Mengele" stands forever as a testament to the evil tortures to which "medical treatment" can be turned.

Treatment or punishment?

85. Even when there is no evil or punitive intent, the patient cannot always tell the difference. It may be a pretty legal theory, but perhaps the Justices who have Decided that medical treatment cannot be punishment have never heard the agonized cries and pleading of a burn patient having dead skin physically peeled off, or chemically with bleach. Perhaps they have never had their crushed bones regularly rubbed together during log rolls, while painkiller was restricted and withheld. Or listened to the whimpering of an Aunt forced to die of ovarian cancer without painkiller. Or been subjected to forced drugging, intimidation and humiliation in a mental "hospital".

86. Sometimes the only difference between torture and treatment is a legal definition; to the person suffering abuse and agony it's all the same.

---

process petitions for sterilization. These courts allowed a broad range of citizens to propose that an individual should be sterilized."

[151] Claude Moore Health Sciences Library, 2004, Carrie Buck Revisited | Eugenics: Three Generations, No Imbeciles, U. of Virginia, http://exhibits.hsl.virginia.edu/eugenics/5-epilogue/,

"The United States Supreme Court affirmed Virginia's sterilization law on May 2, 1927, and the constitutionality of that ruling has never been challenged nor has the ruling ever been overturned. In Virginia repealed the 1924 sterilization law in 1974, while compulsory sterilization of those with "hereditary forms of mental illness that are recurrent" was a part of the Virginia Code until 1979. In the late 1990s, pressure was exerted on the Virginia State Assembly to acknowledge the injustice of the sterilization law after historians and reporters drew clear links between the Virginia law and the enthusiasm shown for eugenics by Nazi Germany."

This Court's eugenics and mental health Decisions have:

a-   Gone so far as to justify and enable torture in the name of "treatment", even of an

child in a mental facility named after a Judge [152] ;

b-   Caused between 60,000 and 70,000 persons, up into the 1970s, mostly poor and

colored [153] [154], to be forcibly sterilized on the basis of social prejudice and the junk

science of eugenics, which Hitler used to begin the Holocaust with a German

sterilization act, modeled precisely on the Virginia Act validated by this Court in 1927

(Buck v. Bell), and never overturned [155] [156] [157] ;

---

[152] Electric Shocks Are Inhumane And Barbaric, http://www.cchrflorida.org/blog/electric-shocks-areinhumane-and-barbaric/ and http://www.youtube.com/watch?v=RlJ10qnrfl4&

[153] Stern, Alexandra Minna, 2005, "Sterilized in the name of public health: Race, Immigration, and Reproductive Control in Modern California", American Journal of Public Health | July 2005, Vol 95, No. 7, 1128-1138

[154] Virginia Eugenics http://www.uvm.edu/~lkaelber/eugenics/VA/VA.html

[155] Grodin, Michael and George Annas, 2007, Physicians and torture: lessons from the Nazi doctors, Int'l Review of the Red Cross, Volume 89 Number 867 September 2007,

   "The idea of racial hygiene emerged at the turn of the twentieth century, and the racial policies of
the Third Reich were in many ways adapted from eugenics practices developed in the United States in
the early twentieth century.12"

   "In the US Supreme Court decision Buck v. Bell, referring to the fact that the state can draft
people into military service, the Court concluded,

   We have seen more than once that the public welfare may call upon the best
   citizens for their lives. It would be strange if it could not call upon those who
   already sap the strength of the State for these lesser sacrifices, often not felt to
   be such by those concerned, in order to prevent our being swamped with
   incompetence. It is better for all the world, if instead of waiting to
   execute degenerate offspring for crime, or to let them starve for their
   imbecility, society can prevent those who are manifestly unfit from continuing
   their kind. The principle that sustains compulsory vaccination is broad
   enough to cover cutting the Fallopian tubes. Three generations of imbeciles
   are enough.14
   Ultimately, the Nazis would carry this ideology beyond sterilization."

c- Wrongfully assumed due process protections which this Court could never

guarantee [158] [159] [160] [161] [162] [163] [164] [165], including "proof more substantial than a mere

---

"Their mission began with the elimination of disabled persons. Psychiatrists and psychoanalysts played a major role in the killing of as many as 100,000 mentally and physically disabled persons between 1939 and 1941"

"Genetic Health Courts were created to decide who ought to be sterilized, and by the end of the Nazi regime had ordered the forced sterilization of over 400,000 people"

"We are all the potential victims of physicians who have become human rights outlaws. But the individuals who have suffered torture or cruel and inhuman treatment facilitated by them or actually ordered or conducted by them deserve more than simply having those outlaws brought to justice. They deserve not only a public acknowledgment of the unlawful and unethical abuse inflicted on them, but also just compensation for their injuries."

[156] Lombardo, Paul A., 2002, "The American Breed": Nazi Eugenics and the Origins of the Pioneer Fund, Albany Law Review, Vol. 65, No. 3, 2002, discussing the intimate connections between American and German /Nazi eugenics through the Pioneer Fund.

[157] Mehler, Barry, 1987, 'Eliminating the Inferior: American and Nazi Sterilization Programs,' *Science for the People* (Nov-Dec 1987) pp. 14-18,

"The Nazi sterilization law was promulgated on July 14, 1933. Within two months, the *Eugenical News* printed a major evaluation of the law, including its complete text in translation. The Nazi government was praised for being the 'first of the world's major nations to enact a modern sterilization law.' The German law 'reads almost like' Harry Laughlin's 'American model sterilization law,' and along with the American statutes was expected to 'constitute a milestone' (sic) in the movement to control human reproduction."

[158] Akin, John Warren, 2009, Inherited Realities: Eugenics, Oliver Wendell Holmes, Jr., and *Buck v. Bell*, *The Tower*, Vol 1, Number 2, Spring 2009, arguing that Justice Holmes' unwarranted dependence upon procedural protections which he could not guarantee allowed the involuntary sterilization of over 60,000 U.S. citizens and the loss of their future generations [as well as helping start the Nazi Holocaust].

[159] Addington v. Texas, 1979, 441 U.S. 418, in which Mr. Justice Burgher wrongfully assumed that "layers of review" and "concern of family and friends" would be sufficient to guarantee due process, and presumed, without any personal knowledge or experience with the effects and stigma of civil commitment that the committing an innocent and harmless person could be no worse than letting a mentally ill person go without "treatment", the likes of which Mr. Justice Burgher had not experienced himself, thus setting in

motion the eventual false commitment of hundreds of thousands of harmless and innocent people in psychiatric hospital insurance scams, including children below the age of five.

> "The heavy standard applied in criminal cases manifests our concern that the risk of error to the individual must be minimized even at the risk that some who are guilty might go free. *Patterson v. New York,* 432 U. S. 197, 432 U. S. 208 (1977). The full force of that idea does not apply to a civil commitment. It may be true that an erroneous commitment is sometimes as undesirable as all erroneous conviction, 5 J. Wigmore, Evidence § 1400 (Chadbourn rev.1974). However, even though an erroneous confinement should be avoided in the first instance, the layers of professional review and observation of the patient's condition, and the concern of family and [Page 441 U. S. 429] friends generally will provide continuous opportunities for an erroneous commitment to be corrected. Moreover, it is not true that the release of a genuinely mentally ill person is no worse for the individual than the failure to convict the guilty. One who is suffering from a debilitating mental illness and in need of treatment is neither wholly at liberty nor free of stigma. *See* Chodoff, The Case for Involuntary Hospitalization of the Mentally Ill, 133 Am.J.Psychiatry 496, 498 (1976); Schwartz, Myers, & Astrachan, Psychiatric Labeling and the Rehabilitation of the Mental Patient, 31 Arch.Gen.Psychiatry 329, 334 (1974). It cannot be said, therefore, that it is much better for a mentally ill person to "go free" than for a mentally normal person to be committed."

[160] Usahacharoenporn, Proud, 2011, E.P. v. Alaska Psychiatric Institute: The Evolution of Involuntary Civil Commitments from Treatment to Punishment, Alaska Law Rev., 28(1):189-216, citing a person committed to the Alaska Psychiatric Institute for 10 months for huffing gasoline, without any treatment for his addiction,

> "E.P. was wrongfully committed for three reasons. First, he was more likely gravely disabled than a danger to himself; however, he could not be committed for being gravely disabled because the State could not show that his condition would improve with treatment. Second, the State did not meet its burden of proving that E.P. was a danger to himself. Third, even if E.P. was a danger to himself, the Alaska Statutes require the State to show that he would improve with treatment."

[161] Madrigal v Quilligan, 9th Cir, 639 F.2d 789 (1978), brought by ten women who claimed that they had been coerced into being sterilized, including by one doctor who allegedly said, ""poor minority women in L.A. County were having too many babies; that it was a strain on society; and that it was good to be sterilized." [see Rubin, 2012], with which the Judge apparently agreed, claiming that the doctors involved sterilized the women for their own good (Third and Fourth Principles of Oppression). When this Court leaves the door open to abusing civil liberties and due process, without penalty or accountability, bigots will walk through in their tens of thousands, trampling the Constitution under this Court's blind eyes.

[162] Rubin, Nilmini Gunaratne, 2012, A crime against motherhood - Involuntary sterilization was a horrifying exercise in genetic engineering, Los Angeles Times, May 13, 2012, http://articles.latimes.com/2012/may/13/opinion/la-oe-rubin-eugenics-mothers-day-20120513, written by a woman whose Sri Lankan mother was sterilized over her objections, after giving birth to her one and only child, because the white doctor felt, "there are too many colored babies already." Considering the millions lost to generations of involuntary sterilization, and the millions more unjustly committed for financial gain, this Court should declare un-Consitutional any law which can be abused without accounting.

[163] Akin, John Warren, 2009, Inherited Realities: Eugenics, Oliver Wendell Holmes, Jr., and *Buck v. Bell*, *The Tower*, Vol 1, Number 2, Spring 2009,

> "By leaving these patients on their own to prove that they ought not to be sterilized in the face of a machine few understood and even fewer could fight, the law effectively abandoned these citizens and irrevocably altered their lives in the most fundamental of ways."

[By the same token, those involuntarily committed have also been left to prove the negative.]

[164] Virginia Eugenics, circa 2008, http://www.uvm.edu/~lkaelber/eugenics/VA/VA.html

> "Virginians were able to modernize their identity while maintaining the purity of their state through the coerced sterilization of minorities and undesirable whites alike (Dorr 2000, p. 262). Often, "mongrels" and "worthless" whites were collected in "mountain sweeps." This involved a sheriff of a nearby town driving into mountain villages and forcibly removing individuals and taking them to institutions where they would only be released upon submission to sterilization (Black 2003, pp. 3-8). More often than not these individuals were unaware of the consequences of the procedures that they underwent." [So much for the protections of due process that Justice Holmes and this Court have assumed.]

[165] Nilsson, Kevin, circa 2000, Eugenics: A Historical Analysis, http://campus.udayton.edu/~hume/Eugenics/eugenics.htm

> "Nowhere is the social effect of sterilization more prevalent than with the story of Howard Hale. Howard Hale was the proprietor for a small candy store that catered to the "misfit" families of the mountains of Virginia during the 1930s. He recalled how state sterilization authorities would literally round up whole "misfit" families. "Everybody who was drawing from welfare then was scared they were going to have it done on them. They were hiding all through these mountains, and the sheriff and his men had to go up after them…They really got them up on Brush Mountain. The sheriff went up there and loaded all of them in a couple of cars and ran them down to Staunton so they could sterilize them." Hale added that "people as a whole were very much in favor of what was going on. They couldn't see more people coming into the world to get on the welfare." (Kevles, 116)"

preponderance of the evidence"[166], which this Court then utterly overthrew in

Barefoot v. Estelle (1983) by allowing prejudicial hypothetical questions[167][168], and

"expert evidence" with a probability of error worse than flipping a coin[169], against the

advice of the medical organization responsible for vetting such "expert predictions",

---

[Again, the complete breakdown of due process due to the bigotry endorsed and enabled by this Court, in a Decision that has never been overturned. There is "no convincing evidence" this is entirely unlike the psychiatric hospitals in Texas paying bounties to outside security firms to drag people in off the street to fill their beds with patients covered by insurance.]

[166] Addington v. Texas, 1979, 441 U.S. 418,

"The individual's liberty interest in the outcome of a civil commitment proceeding is of such weight and gravity, compared with the state's interests in providing care to its citizens who are unable, because of emotional disorders, to care for themselves and in protecting the community from the dangerous tendencies of some who are mentally ill, that due process requires the state to justify confinement by proof more substantial than a mere preponderance of the evidence. Pp. 441 U. S. 425-427."

[167] Barefoot v. Estelle, 1983, 463 U.S. 880, "Psychiatric testimony need not be based on personal examination of the defendant, but may properly be given in response to hypothetical questions."

[168] Fitzsimons, GJ and B. Shiv, 2001, Nonconscious and Contaminative Effects of Hypothetical Questions on Subsequent Decision Making, JOURNAL OF CONSUMER RESEARCH, Inc., Vol. 28, September 2001, pp 224-38,

"In this article we examine the impact of asking hypothetical questions on respondents' subsequent decision making. Across several experiments we find that even though such questions are purely hypothetical, respondents are unable to prevent a substantial biasing effect on their behavior. Further, we find that an increase in cognitive elaboration increases the contaminative effects of hypothetical questions and that this increase occurs primarily when the hypothetical information is relevant. In-depth poststudy interviews with a subset of the participants suggest that the effects of hypothetical questions on choice occur beyond awareness and, as a result, are quite difficult to counteract."

[169] Barefoot v. Estelle, 463 U.S. 880 (1983),

"Nor, despite the view of the American Psychiatric Association supporting petitioner's view, is there any convincing evidence that such testimony is almost entirely unreliable"

merely for the purpose of putting a single prisoner to death [170], regardless of the consequences to society at large [see multiple references cited on psychiatric hospital insurance scams];

d-   Created a sub-class of citizen in those with and without mental illness, subject to unequal and reduced rights in court proceedings, and legal humiliation and intimidation in mental institutions, often merely to coerce "patients" into "appropriate behavior", or strip them of medical insurance [171 172 173 174 175 176 177 178 179 180 181 182 183 184];

---

[170] Appelbaum, P.S., 1984, The Supreme Court looks at psychiatry, Am. J. Psychiatry, 141(7):827-35, July 1984, cites this Court's changing "rhetoric about psychiatry" from 1975 to 1983 in order to justify agendas "outside the realm of mental health law"

[171] Grodin, Michael and George Annas, 2007, Physicians and torture: lessons from the Nazi doctors, Int'l Review of the Red Cross, Volume 89 Number 867 September 2007,

   "Ten years after Milgram's landmark work, Philip Zimbardo simulated prison life among college students in the famous Prison Experiment at Stanford University, randomly assigning housemates to be either a guard or a prisoner. Within six days,the subjects had changed from university students who were friends and roommates to abusive controlling guards and servile prisoners.35 Prisoners became passive, dependent and helpless. Guards expressed feelings of power and group belonging."

[172] Boodman, Sandra, 1992, Ads for Psychiatric Hosptials Come Under Attack, The Washington Post, May 08, 1992

[173] Deneen, Sally, 1988, Complaints about psychiatric hospitals rise, August 19, 1988, Sun-Sentinel, Florida

[174] Erlinder,C. Peter, 2003, Essay: Of Rights Lost and Rights Found: The Coming Restoration of the Right to a Jury Trial in Minnesota Civil Commitment Proceedings, 29 Wm. Mitchell L. Rev. 1269

[175] Mohr, Wanda K., 1998, Experiences of patients hospitalized during the Texas mental health scandal, Perspectives in Psychiatric Care, Vol 34, 1998

[176] Nadler, Art, 1998, Several claim they've been hospitalized against their will, Las Vegas Sun, Jan 24, 1998

e-   Damaged of tens of thousands of innocent and harmless people in the State of

Texas alone [185] , including children below the age of five [186], by giving psychiatrists

the unaccountable power to unilaterally decide that any person needs their treatment;

---

[177] Olberg, Becky, 2011, The Abuse of Psychiatric Detention and Its Complications, http://www.healthyplace.com/blogs/borderline/2011/02/the-abu..., *Posted on February 15, 2011,* noting the threat and false use of psychiatric detention for such things as preventing the spread of pink eye.

[178] Rappaport, Richard G., MD, 2006, Losing Your Rights: Complications of Misdiagnosis, J Am Acad Psychiatry Law 34:4:436-438 (December 2006), noting the use of commitment in one case to suppress political activism

[179] Sileo, Chi Chi, 1994, Rip-off depress mental health care – fraud in psychiatric hospital practices, Insight on the News, Jan 24, 1994

[180] Smith, Mark, 1991, PROFITABLE ADDICTIONS/Captured and held against will/Some private hospitals prey on patients with insurance, Houston Chronicle 09/09/1991

[181] Smith, Mark, 1992, Profitable Addictions/Abuses in mental health programs are pinpointed, Houston Chronicle. 04/29/1992, Section A, p 1,2

[182] Smith, Mark, 1993a, Profitable Addictions/Doctor who triggered probe claims he's scapetgoat, Houston Chronicle, 07/18/1993 Section State, p 1,2

[183] Smith, Mark, 1993b, State probes psychiatric care of youth Morales checks into legality of expensive hospitalizations, Houston Chronicle, 11/21/1993

[184] Langel, et al., 2003, Psychiatric commitment – patients perspectives, Med Law. 2003;22(1):39-53

[185] Smith, Mark, et al., Houston Chronicle "Profitable Addictions" series, at least 42 articles during the period of about 5/14/1989 to 3/24/1997, on tens of thousands of false commitments in the State of Texas.

[186] Smith, Mark & Rugley, Cindy, 1993, State probes psychiatric care of youth Morales checks into legality of expensive hospitalizations, 1/21/1993 Houston Chronicle, Sect A, pg 1,2,

    "in the most recent fiscal year," "205 children from ages 1 to 5", "2,272 children ages 6 to 14", "September 1992-August 1993........3,339 [commitments]........$ 69,460,334"

    "Texas is apparently not the only state facing these problems." "A letter from the Health Care Financing Authority, the federal agency responsible for Medicaid, said a study of Oklahoma and Louisiana found that 25 percent and 32 percent of sampled children were "inappropriately admitted."" ""I can think of almost no circumstances where a 2-year-old should be in a psychiatric hospital. That's been a problem and I think the state recognizes that," said Dr. Mike McKinney, a former state

f- Cost the U.S. Government millions of dollars in bogus payments for unjustified

psychiatric diagnoses and commitments specifically directed at military families with

rich medical benefits[187] [188] ;

g- Caused deleterious effects upon even those with severe hallucinations [189],

including tremors indistinguishable from the brain damage of Parkinson's disease [190] [191]

[192] [193];

---

representative who is now medical director of National Heritage Insurance Co., which contracts with the state to administer Medicaid payments."

"Federal reports have warned that Medicaid and other federal funds could be ripe for misuse by psychiatric facilities looking for additional revenue sources." ""Because of the adverse publicity that psychiatric hospitals have received, as well as increased scrutiny by insurance companies, some hospital occupancy rates are down, placing pressure on them to generate more revenue," a federal General Accounting Office report warned in September."

[187] Kerr, Peter, April 29, 1992, Government review finds 64% of psychiatric hospital stays aren't needed, New York Times News Service / Baltimore Sun

[188] Smith, Mark, 1992, Profitable Addictions/Abuses in mental health programs are pinpointed, Houston Chronicle. 04/29/1992, Section A, p 1,2, "One-third of the more than $600 million in mental health claims filed by military employees and their dependents in fiscal 1990 were "medically unnecessary," a General Accounting Office study indicates"

[189] Gray, Benjamin, 2009, Psychiatry and Oppression: A Personal Account of Compulsory Admission and Medical Treatment, Schizophrenia Bulletin, 2009 - as can be reasonably extrapolated to U.S. facilities (see One Flew Over the Cuckoo's Nest by Ken Kesey, based upon his experience in at least one US facility)

[190] Washington v. Harper, 494 U.S. 210 (1990), Justice Stevens:

"As with all psychotropic drugs, prolixin may cause tardive dyskinesia, an often irreversible syndrome of uncontrollable movements that can prevent a person from exercising basic functions such as driving an automobile, and neuroleptic malignant syndrome, which is 30% fatal for those who suffer from it. [Footnote 2/7] The risk of side effects increases over time. [Footnote 2/8]"

[191] Perlin, Micheal L., 1991, Competency, Deinstitutionalization, And Homelessness: A Story Of Marginalization, 28 Hous. L. Rev. 63,

h- caused matter-of-course denials of civil rights and due process in "civil"

commitments[194] [195] [196];

citing Rennie v. Klein, 476 F. Supp. 1294, 1299-1300 (D.N.J. 1979), at 1146 (remarking that the likelihood of a patient contracting tardive dyskinesia raises the question of whether "the cure would be worse than the illness"); Bellack & Mueser, *supra* note 164, at 177 (asserting that as many as 50% of schizophrenics may not benefit from antipsychotic medication, and that it does not help patients "develop skills of daily living that enhance the quality of life"). *See generally* Diamond, *Drugs and the Quality of Life: The Patient's Point of View,* 46 J. CLINICAL PSYCHIATRY 29 (1985);

and "As Judge Stanley Brotman noted over a decade ago in *Rennie v. Klein,* [FN240] the same drugs prescribed to lessen the severity of thought disorders also served to "inhibit a patient's ability to learn social skills needed to fully recover from psychosis . . . . " [FN241] Side effects such as akinesia and akathesia [FN242] have the inevitable effect of retarding social skill progress and of making expatients even less employable once they are deinstitutionalized. [FN243] While the drugs may be effective in reducing the floridity of symptomatology and lessening the excesses of psychic pain, [FN244] no one--neither the patients' rights advocates, the spokespersons for the APA, nor the deinstitutionalization theorists--has yet critically considered the linkage between these drug side effects, the failure *105 of patients to be meaningfully reintegrated into society after their release, and homelessness. [FN245] The linkage is especially pernicious in light of the parallel literature illuminating the ways in which institutional dependency progressively leads to losses of social and vocational competencies, *precisely* the sort of "competencies" that are essential if homeless individuals are to reintegrate themselves meaningfully into mainstream society. [FN246]"

[192] Brown, Katherine & Erin Murphy, *Falling Through the Cracks: The Quebec Mental Health System,* 45 MCGILL L.J. 1037, 1062 (2000).

[A] significant disadvantage to the use of such drugs is the side effects suffered **by** those who take these medications over a prolonged period ... [The more serious and enduring side effects are the movement or neuromuscular disorders] the most prevalent one being *tardive dyskinesia.* This disorder ... is generally thought to be untreatable and irreversible. It may present itself in the form of involuntary movements of the tongue, mouth or cheeks; similarly it may cause bizarre, involuntary movements of the torso or limbs . . . While clinical studies on the prevalence of these side effects . .. yield various results, the incidence . .. is not insignificant.

[193] Gottstein, James B., 2008, Involuntary commitment and forced psychiatric drugging in the trial courts: rights violations as a matter of course, Alaska Law Review, Vol. 25:51-105

[194] Gottstein, James B., 2008, Involuntary commitment and forced psychiatric drugging in the trial courts: rights violations as a matter of course, Alaska Law Review, Vol. 25:51-105, "*By abandoning their core*

principle of zealous advocacy,lawyers representing psychiatric respondents interpose little, if any, defense and are not discovering and presenting to judges the evidence of the harm to their clients."

"The distinction between scientific evidence requiring a "*Coon/Daubert* analysis" and experience-based expertise which does not is a critical one, because the psychiatrists called by the hospital in favor of involuntary commitment and forced drugging petitions are asked to provide expert opinions in both categories.[214] Instead of any recognition of the distinction, they are uniformly qualified as "experts in psychiatry" and allowed to testify with respect to scientific knowledge without compliance with *Coon*.[215]"

[195] Stevens, Lawrence, J.D. circa 2000, Unjustified Psychiatric Commitment in the U.S.A., www.antipsychiatry.org. "The invalidity and unreliability of psychiatric "diagnosis", often complicated by the psychiatrist's financial stake in getting the so-called patient committed, combined with the immutable reluctance of most judges to use their own independent judgment, makes a jury absolutely essential for a fair trial in psychiatric commitment cases. This is truly a case of "NO JURY - NO JUSTICE"."

2000 UPDATE

"The confusing aspect about this is that many adolescents are irritable, aggressive, and impulsive because they are upset about their life circumstances. In recent years some of these teenagers have found their way into psychiatric hospitals, labeled with the diagnosis of bipolar disorder and placed on medications. Some psychiatric hospitals made a practice of admitting adolescents in distress, using the diagnosis of bipolar disorder inappropriately in order to increase their billing to insurance companies. This practice was so widespread that the federal government finally intervened, charging the hospitals with fraud and assessing fines of millions of dollars. Many of these children did not have bipolar disorder at all, but were acting inappropriately because of stresses in their families, with their friends, and at school." Edward Drummond, M.D., Associate Medical Director at Seacoast Mental Health Center in Portsmouth, New Hampshire, in his book *The Complete Guide to Psychiatric Drugs* (John Wiley & Sons, Inc., New York, 2000), pages 13-14. Dr. Drummond graduated from Tufts University School of Medicine and was trained in psychiatry at Harvard University.

[196] Perlin, Michael L., 1994, *The ADA and Persons with Mental Disabilities: Can Sanist Attitudes Be Undone?* by Journal of Law and Health, 1993/1994, 8 JLHEALTH 15, 27p,

"Courts and legislatures often respond to these sanist attitudes by condoning (or encouraging) pretextuality in both civil and criminal cases involving litigants with mental disabilities."

"Rarely, if ever, is behavioral or scientific authority cited to support sanist opinions. At least one court, without citation to any authority, has found that it is less likely that medical patients will "fabricate descriptions of their complaints" than will "psychological patients." [FN91] Another court has likened

i-   In Buck v. Bell, 1927, used unscientific arguments to create unnecessarily broad

consequences, to justify sterilizing as an "imbecile" an unwed mother, who was a

good student[197] and raped by a member of her foster family [198] [199] [200] [201], which spread

---

the accuracy inherent in psychiatric predictivity of future dangerousness to predictions made by an

oncologist as to consequences of an untreated and metastasized malignancy. [FN92] This unsubstantiated

analysis made in spite of the *32 overwhelming weight of clinical and behavioral literature which

concludes that psychiatrists are far more often incorrect in predicting dangerousness than they are

accurate. [FN93] Yet another court has rejected expert testimony on a homicide defendant's reactions to

fear and stress on the grounds that such emotions are "experienced by all mankind" and were thus not

related to any body of scientific knowledge. [FN94]"

"The entire relationship between the legal process and litigants with mental disabilities is often

pretextual. By this I mean simply that courts accept (either implicitly or explicitly) testimonial

dishonesty, and engage similarly in dishonest (frequently meretricious) decision making, specifically

where witnesses, especially *expert* witnesses, show a "high propensity to purposely distort their

testimony in order to achieve desired ends." [FN95] This pretextuality is poisonous. Its toxin infects all

participants in the judicial system, breeds cynicism and disrespect for the law, demeans participants, and

reinforces shoddy lawyering, blase judging, and, at times, perjurious and/or corrupt testifying. The

reality is well known to frequent consumers of judicial services in this area: to mental health advocates

and other public defender/legal aid/legal service lawyers assigned to represent patients and criminal

defendants who are mentally disabled, to prosecutors and state attorneys assigned to represent hospitals,

to judges who regularly hear such cases, to expert and lay witnesses, and, most importantly, to the person

with a mental disability involved in the litigation in question."

[197] "Three Generations of Imbeciles"?, http://www.facinghistory.org/three-generations-imbeciles, From

Race and Membership in American History: The Eugenics Movement, Chapter 6,

"A simple check of state records would have revealed that Emma Buck and her husband were legally

married at the time Carrie was born, although they separated when she was very young. Unable to

support Carrie after she and her husband parted, Emma placed the four-year-old in foster care. The child

was sent to live with a Mr. and Mrs. J. T. Dobbs. She did chores for the couple and attended school

through the sixth grade. She kept up with her classmates and was promoted every year. According to

school records, her sixth-grade teacher characterized Buck's work and behavior as "very good.""

[198] Buck v. Bell, 2013, from Wikipedia, http://en.wikipedia.org/wiki/Buck_v._Bell,

sterilization laws across the States and across Oceans, to support some of the worst

excesses of the 20th century, including the Holocaust, and the sterilization of primarily

poor and colored people here in the U.S., even without their knowledge or consent,

extending into the 1970s (see references cited previously and elsewhere);

"In the summer of 1923, while her adoptive mother was away "on account of some illness," her adoptive mother's nephew raped Carrie, and Carrie's later commitment has been seen as an attempt by the family to save their reputation."

[199] "Three Generations of Imbeciles"?, http://www.facinghistory.org/three-generations-imbeciles, From Race and Membership in American History: The Eugenics Movement, Chapter 6,

"In the early 1920s, a nephew of Mrs. Dobbs joined the household, possibly to help with farm work much as Buck helped with the housework. In the summer of 1923, when Buck was about 16, the nephew raped her while his aunt and uncle were away from home."

[200] Claude Moore Health Sciences Library, 2004, Buck v. Bell - Eugenics_ Three Generations, No Imbeciles_ Virginia, Eugenics & Buck v. Bell, http://exhibits.hsl.virginia.edu/eugenics/3-buckvbell/

"Carrie Buck's foster parents had committed her to the Virginia Colony shortly after she gave birth to an illegitimate child. The family's embarrassment may have been compounded by the fact that Carrie's pregnancy was the result of being raped by a relative of her foster parents. This point was never raised in the subsequent court proceedings."

[201] Virginia Eugenics, circa 2008, http://www.uvm.edu/~lkaelber/eugenics/VA/VA.html

"Buck was classified as "feeble-minded" after giving birth to an illegitimate child as a result of rape by relative of her foster family. Her daughter was subsequently deemed feebleminded at the age of 6 months.

"Under accusations of hereditary defectiveness, Carrie Buck faced a series of trials and appeals used to legitimize her pending sterilization. She was defended by Aubrey Strode, a known supporter of sterilization, whose defense focused more on the potential benefits of Buck's sterilization than the consequences (Lombardo 2008b, p. 136) Nonetheless, with the 1927 Supreme Court ruling in Buck v. Bell, sterilization was legitimized and Buck was consequently sterilized to prevent the birth of more "defective" individuals."

j-   In Barefoot v. Estelle, 1983, created unnecessarily broad and unscientific

arguments[202][203][204][205] specifically to justify putting a single prisoner to death, which

---

[202] Barefoot v. Estelle - 463 U.S. 880 (1983),

"Nor, despite the view of the American Psychiatric Association supporting petitioner's view, is there any convincing evidence that such testimony is almost entirely unreliable,"

" As indicated above, however, the same view was presented and rejected in *Estelle v. Smith.* We are no more convinced now that the view of the APA should be converted into a constitutional rule barring an entire category of expert testimony. [Footnote 6] We are not persuaded that such testimony is almost entirely unreliable, and that the factfinder and the adversary system will not be competent to uncover, recognize, and take due account of its shortcomings. The *amicus* does not suggest that there are not other views held by members of the Association or of the profession generally. Indeed, as this case and others indicate, there are those doctors who are quite willing to testify at the sentencing hearing, who think, and will say, that they know what they are talking about, and who expressly disagree with the Association's point of view. [Footnote 7] Furthermore, their *Page 463 U. S. 900* qualifications as experts are regularly accepted by the courts. If they are so obviously wrong and should be discredited, there should be no insuperable problem in doing so by calling *Page 463 U. S. 901* members of the Association who are of that view and who confidently assert that opinion in their *amicus* brief. Neither petitioner nor the Association suggests that psychiatrists are always wrong with respect to future dangerousness, only most of the time."

[203] Tolson, Mike, 2004. Effect of "Dr. Death" and his testimony lingers; Doctor's effect on justice lingers/Testified in many death row cases; By Mike Tolson, June 17, 2004, Houston Chronicle,

"Grigson's eagerness to make absolute judgments earned him the praise of prosecutors and the scorn of professional psychiatric organizations. He was twice reprimanded by the American Psychiatric Association, once for using the results of a competency examination against a defendant during the punishment phase of his trial, the other time for claiming 100-percent accuracy in predicting how dangerous a defendant he had never examined would be in future years. The psychiatric establishment considered his opinions little more than quackery. Paul Appelbaum, a University of Massachusetts psychiatry professor whose complaints ultimately led the APA to expel Grigson, complained that future behavior went well beyond what science can purport to know. Grigson, stung by the rebuke, fought the expulsion with a lawsuit, to no avail. He blamed the action on anti-death-penalty doctors in the group. Later the Texas Society of Psychiatric Physicians also booted Grigson from its ranks."

[204] Monahan, John, 6-1-2000, Violence Risk Assessment: Scientific Validity and Evidentiary Admissibility, Washington and Lee Law Rev, Article 8, 57(3):901-918,

"I reviewed research on the accuracy of clinical judgments at predicting the criterion of "violent behavior toward others" in 1981The research concluded that "psychiatrists and psychologists are accurate in no more than one out of three predictions of violent behavior over a several-year period among institutionalized populations that had both committed violence in the past (and thus had high base rates for it) and who were diagnosed as mentally ill. " ° Remarkably, only one study of the validity of clinicians at predicting "violence in the community" was published between 1979 and 1993." This was a study of court-ordered pretrial mental health assessments conducted in 1978.2 Consistent with the previous literature, 39% of the defendants rated by clinicians as having a "high" likelihood for being violent to others were reported to have committed dangerous acts during a two-year follow-up, compared to 26% of defendants considered as having a "low" likelihood, a statistically significant difference.' 3" ...

"There is a long tradition in criminology of using actuarial techniques in predicting recidivism by released prisoners. For example, actuarial predictions are used by statutes to determine parole eligibility in a number of states3 ° Actuarial techniques, however, only recently have been applied to predicting violence among people with mental disorders." ...

"The most recent development in this area is the publication of the work of the MacArthur Violence Risk Assessment Study."0 Here, the researchers developed what they called an "Iterative Classification Tree," or ICT.5' They sought to increase the utility of this actuarial method for real-world clinical decision making **by** applying the method to a set of violence risk factors commonly available in clinical records or capable of being routinely assessed in clinical practice.52 Results showed that the ICT partitioned three-quarters of a sample of psychiatric patients into one of two categories with regard to their risk of violence to others during the first twenty weeks after discharge (a period during which **18.7%** of all patients committed at least one violent act). 3 One category consisted of groups whose rates of violence were no more than half the baserate of the total patient sample (i.e., equal to or less **than** 9% violent). 4 The other category consisted of groups whose rates of violence were *at least twice* the baserate of the total patient sample (i.e., equal to or greater than 37% violent).55 The prevalence of violence within individual risk groups varied from 3% to 53%, considerably more accurate than clinical prediction 56" ...

"I note at the outset that the leading American legal treatise in this field, Modem Scientific Evidence: The Law and Science of Expert Testimony, states:

> To date, no court has evaluated the admissibility of expert testimony regarding future violence under the Court's recent *Daubert* decision. In light of the very few cases preceding Daubert which engaged in any evidentiary analysis whatsoever, this state of affairs is unlikely to change soon."' ...

have spread into civil commitment procedures, resulting in the unnecessary

commitment of hundreds of thousands of harmless and innocent people [206] [207];

"Commenting on the inevitable margin of error in predicting human behavior, Faigman and others concluded as did the *Benchbook.* "Although courts appear to uniformly accept the inherent difficulty in predicting future behavior, they have, nonetheless, liberally permitted expert testimony on this issue. 80 … Given all this, it is hlghly unlike that the Daubert decision will affect the admissibility of professional assessments of dangerousness in federal courts or in states that follow the *Daubert* ecision.'°""

[205] Monahan, et al., 2001-2005, MacArthur Risk Assessment Study,

"*Creating Different Cut-Offs for High and Low Risk.* Rather than relying on the standard single threshold for distinguishing among cases, we decided to employ two thresholds – one for identifying higher risk cases and one for identifying lower risk cases. We assumed that inevitably there will be cases that fall between these two thresholds, cases for which any actuarial prediction scheme is incapable of making an adequate assessment of high or low risk. The degree of risk presented by these intermediate cases cannot be statistically distinguished from the base rate of the sample as a whole (therefore, we refer to these cases as constituting an "average risk" group)." …

"Using only the 106 risk factors commonly available in hospital records or capable of being routinely assessed in clinical practice, we were able to place all patients into one of five risk classes for which the prevalence of violence during the first 20 weeks following discharge into the community varied between 1 percent and 76 percent. The risk factors that emerged most frequently on the various models are presented in Table 1,"

[206] Smith, Mark and others, circa 1989-1997, "Profitable Addictions" newspaper series, The Houston Chronicle

[207] See also footnote references for Question 4

k-   Despite its previous concern with "erroneous commitment"[208], effectively

upended the legal principle of "innocent until proven guilty" in mental health issues[209]

to something worse than Stalin's alleged maxim, "Better that ten innocent men suffer

than one spy escape", as demonstrated in the Statement of the Case;

l-   Created unequal applications of law and deprivations of freedom of speech[210], on

the unconstitutional principle that fear of threat from a person with or perceived to

have mental illness equals threat and violent action from criminal behavior, such that

a white supremacist may freely advocate terrorism [211], but a person with a mental

illness may not speak even of lethal and legitimate self-defense in response to any

---

[208] Addington v. Texas, 441 U.S. 418 (1979), "Since the preponderance standard creates the risk of increasing the number of individuals erroneously committed, it is at least unclear to what extent, if any, the state's interests are furthered by using a preponderance standard in such commitment proceedings."

[209] Barefoot v. Estelle, 463 U.S. 880 (1983),

"(a) There is no merit to petitioner's argument that psychiatrists, individually and as a group, are incompetent to predict with an acceptable degree of reliability that a particular criminal will commit other crimes in the future, and so represent a danger to the community. To accept such an argument would call into question predictions of future behavior that are constantly made in other contexts. Moreover, under the generally applicable rules of evidence covering the admission and weight of unprivileged evidence, psychiatric testimony predicting dangerousness may be countered not only as erroneous in a particular case but also as generally so unreliable that it should be ignored. Nor, despite the view of the American Psychiatric Association supporting petitioner's view, is there any convincing evidence that such testimony is almost entirely unreliable, and that the factfinder and the adversary system will not be competent to uncover, recognize, and take due account of its shortcomings."

[210] Amendment 1

[211] U.S.A v. Stone, et al., Fed. Dist. Ct. MIED, 2:10-cr-20123-VAR-PJK, (3/27/2012, Hutaree militia), white supremacists discussing murdering police and bombing the funeral processions declared freedom of speech

feared criminal assault without preemptive suppression [212]; such that a drug-dealing gangbanger may not be arrested for threats until he actually shoots someone, but any person with a mental illness that the gangbanger threatened may be summarily committed on the complaint of the gangbanger, that the person with a mental illness responded with a "threat" of lethal self-defense; that is the way that State laws such as OSC Title 43A are interpreted in practice;

m-   Enabled unequal distinctions between acts of mass murder and terror according to race and religion, as recent history shows, such that Muslim perpetrators are labeled "terrorists", Black perpetrators are labeled criminals, and nominally-Christian white perpetrators are labeled "mentally ill", thus biasing the entire social and legal perception of mental illness, race and religion;

n-   While recognizing that adult conviction and juvenile delinquency carry equal stigma and require equal procedural safeguards and standards of proof [213] [214] [215],

---

[212] Oklahoma State Code Title 43A, Section 1-103, Definitions, declaring that any persons with a mental illness who is alleged to "having placed another person or persons in a reasonable fear of violent behavior", by verbal or other threats, requires "treatment", while excluding anyone who is elderly and mentally incapacitated, mentally retarded, has a seizure disorder, has a traumatic brain injury, or is homeless.

[213] Winship, 397 U.S. 358, 1970 (see below)

[214] Lessard v. Schmidt, 349 F. Supp. 1078 – Dist. Court, ED Wisconsin (1972),

"At least one court would require proof beyond a reasonable doubt on all questions relating to civil commitment. Denton v. Commonwealth, 383 S.W.2d 681 (Ky.1964). In In re Winship, 397 U.S. 358, 90 S.Ct. 1068, 25 L.Ed.2d 368 (1970), the Supreme Court held that proof beyond a reasonable doubt was required to prove every fact necessary in juvenile delinquency proceedings, noting that "extreme caution in factfinding," *id.* at 365, 90 S.Ct. 1068, is necessary because of "the possibility that [the individual] may lose his liberty upon conviction and because of the certainty that he would be stigmatized by the conviction." *Id.* at 363, 90 S.Ct. at 1072. The Court reiterated its previous holding in

allowed the lower courts, legislatures[216] and psychiatry combined free reign to establish unequal legal and "medical" treatments according to race and insurance status [217][218];

In re Gault, 387 U.S. 1, 87 S.Ct. 1428, 18 L.Ed. 2d 527 (1966), that "civil labels and good intentions do not themselves obviate the need for criminal due process safeguards in juvenile courts, for `[a] proceeding where the issue is whether the child will be found to be "delinquent" and subjected to the loss of his liberty for years is comparable in seriousness to a felony prosecution.'" In re Winship, *supra*, 397 U.S. at 365-366, 90 S.Ct. at 1073.[25] The *Winship* Court reached its conclusion despite its findings that an adjudication of delinquency "does not deprive the child of his civil rights, and that juvenile proceedings are confidential." *Id.* at 366, 90 S.Ct. at 1074.

"The argument for a stringent standard of proof is more compelling in the case of a civil commitment in which an individual will be deprived of basic civil rights and be certainly stigmatized by the lack of confidentiality of the adjudication. We therefore hold that the state must prove beyond a reasonable doubt all facts necessary to show that an individual is mentally ill and dangerous.

"Even if the standards for an adjudication of mental illness and potential dangerousness are satisfied, a court should order full-time involuntary hospitalization only as a last resort. A basic concept in American justice is the principle that "even though the governmental purpose be legitimate and substantial, that purpose cannot be pursued by means that broadly stifle fundamental personal liberties when the end can be more narrowly achieved."

[215] Addington v. Texas, 1979,

"In *Winship,* against the background of a gradual assimilation of juvenile proceedings into traditional criminal prosecutions, we declined to allow the state's "civil labels and good intentions" to "obviate the need for criminal due process safeguards in juvenile courts." 397 U.S. at 397 U. S. 365-366. The Court saw no controlling difference in loss of liberty and stigma between a conviction for an adult and a delinquency adjudication for a juvenile. *Winship* recognized that the basic issue -- whether the individual in fact committed a criminal act – was

Page 441 U. S. 428

the same in both proceedings. There being no meaningful distinctions between the two proceedings, we required the state to prove the juvenile's act and intent beyond a reasonable doubt."

[216] Heller v. Doe, 509 U. S. 312 (1993)

-64-

"Classifications neither involving fundamental rights nor proceeding along suspect lines do not run afoul of the Equal Protection Clause if there is a rational relationship between the disparity of treatment and a legitimate governmental purpose. A legislature need not articulate its rationale, and a State need not produce evidence to sustain the classification's rationality. Moreover, courts are compelled to accept a legislature's generalization even when there is an imperfect fit between means and ends." [A perfect excuse for the prejudiced treatment of people with mental illness.]

[217] Sileo, Chi Chi, 1994, Rip-off depress mental health care – fraud in psychiatric hospital practices, Insight on the News, Jan 24, 1994,

"But a hospital like Stout's, according to Schwartz, may be the exception: "In many of these places, the quality of care is suspect and even abusive," he states. Schwartz cites incidents of children being put in restraints including handcuffs and straitjackets; held in isolation and forbidden from receiving mail or using the phone or having contact with their families; and kept sedated.

"You couldn't get away with treating criminals this way," says Schwartz, who notes that many of these children are under the age of 13. "This whole thing is frightening on many levels. It's a violation of civil rights. It's the medicalization of deviant behavior. And it's racist and elitist. Most of these kids are white and upper middle class; amazingly, there are almost no black or Native American children who are |acting out' or |aggressive' -- just black or Native American children who are assaultive and delinquent. And these children are being tagged with a label and a stigma that will haunt them the rest of their lives."

That last fear is not misplaced. A stay in a psychiatric hospital, even as a child, remains on a person's medical record. And a study by the National Institute of Mental Health in 1993 found that even ex-convicts rank above former mental patients in societal acceptance.

"The stigma is incredible," says a patient. "You can't tell anyone except your most trusted friends. Forget telling an employer! Sometimes they find out anyway, and all of a sudden you're unfit to work there.""

[218] Stevens, Lawrence, J.D. circa 2000, Unjustified Psychiatric Commitment in the U.S.A., www.antipsychiatry.org.

"'It's a hot business,' Tim Goolsby, a Contra Costa County Probation Department adolescent placement supervisor, later agreed. 'If your kids like sex, drugs, and rock'n'roll, that's the place [private mental hospital] to put them. I'm not sure insurance companies know what's going on, but they're being ripped off.' Goolsby estimated 80 percent of adolescents in Contra Costa private psychiatric hospitals are not mentally ill... University of Southern California sociologists Patricia Guttridge and Carol Warren say these adolescents have been transformed from delinquents to emotionally disturbed children. After studying 1,119 adolescents in four Los Angeles-area psychiatric hospitals, they found that less than a

o- Caused unequal treatment under the law between minorities, like unto that addressed in Skinner v. Oklahoma (1942), to wit, minority racial populations, which have demonstrably higher rates of violence than the minority with mental illnesses [219]

---

fifth were admitted for serious mental illnesses" (Susan Stern, *The Tribune* (Oakland, California), Sunday, July 6, 1986, p. A-1 & A-2).

"In the February 1988 *Stanford Law Journal* Lois A. Weithorn, Ph.D., a former University of Virginia psychology professor, said "adolescent admission rates to psychiatric units of private hospitals have jumped dramatically, increasing over four-fold between 1980 and 1984. ... I contend that the rising rates of psychiatric admission of children and adolescents reflect an increasing use of hospitalization to manage a population for whom such intervention is typically inappropriate: 'troublesome' youth who do not suffer from severe mental disorders" (40 Stanford Law Review 773 at 773-774).

"Psychiatric and psychological "diagnosis" is arbitrary and unreliable. Furthermore, the supposed experts responsible for these "diagnoses" are usually biased in favor of commitment because of their personal economic concerns or their affiliation with the psychiatric "hospital" where the "patient" is or will be confined. Psychiatric "hospitals", like all businesses, need customers. In the case of psychiatric "hospitals", they need patients. They not only want patients, they *need* them to stay in business. Similarly, individual psychiatrists and psychologists need patients to make money and earn a living."

[219] Colb, Sherry F., Aug 10, 2011, Armed and Crazy: Should Mentally Ill People Be Permitted to Own Firearms?, Justia.com,

"According to one commonly cited study, 15 percent of people without a major mental disorder report past violent behavior, while 33 percent of people with a serious mental illness report past violent behavior. This statistic means that although the self-reported rate of violence in the "healthy" population is approximately one in six, the corresponding rate of self-reported violence among those with a serious mental illness is twice that, or one in three." ... "it is worth noting that the mentally ill do not make up the only identifiable group of people that carries out more violence, on average, than those outside the group. For a host of reasons, for example, African Americans appear to be **disproportionately involved in committing homicides (http://www.rci.rutgers.edu/~roos/Courses/grstat502/phillipssp802.pdf)** , relative to Whites and relative to Latinos."..."By some accounts, the Black/White disparity is eight-fold, so that the odds that a man will commit a homicide are eight times greater if he is African American, than if he is White." ... "First, the White/Black disparity is four times greater than the mentally-well/mentally-ill disparity, the latter of which is regularly cited as a reason to disarm the mentally ill. Second, and just as significantly, we would rightly reject out of hand the very idea of banning gun ownership on the basis

[220] [221], are given the benefit of the principle innocent until proven guilty and the higher evidentiary protections of criminal law, whereas people with mental illnesses are confined and effectively punished under the less stringent "protections" of civil law, for "inappropriate" speech[222] or action, or the mere suspicion or perception of any tendency of future violent behavior [223] [224], under the principle of dangerous until proven otherwise;

---

of race. Stated differently, though a racially based gun ban would apparently respond to a much more sizable disparity in violence than a mental-illness-based gun ban, we can easily appreciate how offensive and unfair a racially based ban would be." *[note that this "compares" homicide between races with all kinds of violence among those with and without mental illness]*

[220] McCarthy, Kara, 2011, Nov 16, "HOMICIDES FALL TO LOWEST RATE IN FOUR DECADES", U.S. Bureau of Justice Statistics, http://www.bjs.gov/content/pub/press/htus8008pr.cfm,

"Most murders were intraracial. From 1980 through 2008, 84 percent of white homicide victims were murdered by whites and 93 percent of black victims were murdered by blacks. During this same period, blacks were disproportionately represented among homicide victims and offenders. Blacks were six times more likely than whites to be homicide victims and seven times more likely than whites to commit homicide."

[221] Cooper, Alexia and Erica L. Smith, Nov 2011, PATTERNS & TRENDS, Homicide Trends in the United States, 1980-2008, U.S. Bureau of Justice Statistics, NCJ 236018, cites black homicide victimization rate six times whites, offender rate seven times whites in 2008

[222] Amendment 1

[223] Addington v. Texas, 441 U.S. 418 (1979), alleging and citing "the dangerous tendencies of some who are mentally ill"

[224] Kansas v. Hendricks, 521 U.S. 346 (1997), coupling "dangerousness" with "mental illness" as an excuse for commitment: "A finding of dangerousness, standing alone, is ordinarily not a sufficient ground upon which to justify indefinite involuntary commitment. We have sustained civil commitment statutes when they have coupled proof of dangerousness with the proof of some additional factor, such as a "mental illness" or "mental abnormality.""

p-   Further abused those already traumatized by crime, child abuse and violence [225]

[226 227 228 229 230 231 232 233 234] to a much greater extent than the general population [235], by

[225]   Windom, CS, 1999, Posttraumatic stress disorder in abused and neglected children grown up, Am J Psychiatry. 1999 Aug;156(8):1223-9,

"OBJECTIVE: The purpose of this study was to describe the extent to which childhood abuse and neglect increase a person's risk for subsequent posttraumatic stress disorder (PTSD) and to determine whether the relationship to PTSD persists despite controls for family, individual, and lifestyle characteristics associated with both childhood victimization and PTSD. METHOD: Victims of substantiated child abuse and neglect from 1967 to 1971 in a Midwestern metropolitan county area were matched on the basis of age, race, sex, and approximate family socioeconomic class with a group of nonabused and nonneglected children and followed prospectively into young adulthood. Subjects (N = 1,196) were located and administered a 2-hour interview that included the National Institute of Mental Health Diagnostic Interview Schedule to assess PTSD. RESULTS: Childhood victimization was associated with increased risk for lifetime and current PTSD. Slightly more than a third of the childhood victims of sexual abuse (37.5%), 32.7% of those physically abused, and 30.6% of victims of childhood neglect met DSM-III-R criteria for lifetime PTSD. The relationship between childhood victimization and number of PTSD symptoms persisted despite the introduction of covariates associated with risk for both. CONCLUSIONS: Victims of child abuse (sexual and physical) and neglect are at increased risk for developing PTSD, but childhood victimization is not a sufficient condition. Family, individual, and lifestyle variables also place individuals at risk and contribute to the symptoms of PTSD."

[226]   Bierer, LM, et al., 2003, Abuse and neglect in childhood: relationship to personality disorder diagnoses, CNS Spectr. 2003 Oct;8(10):737-54,

"BACKGROUND: Childhood history of abuse and neglect has been associated with personality disorders and has been observed in subjects with lifetime histories of suicidality and self-injury. Most of these findings have been generated from inpatient clinical samples. METHODS: This study evaluated self-rated indices of sustained childhood abuse and neglect in an outpatient sample of well-characterized personality disorder subjects (n=182) to determine the relative associations of childhood trauma indices to specific personality disorder diagnoses or clusters and to lifetime history of suicide attempts or gestures. Subjects met criteria for ~2.5 Axis II diagnoses and 24% reported past suicide attempts. The Childhood Trauma Questionnaire was administered to assess five dimensions of childhood trauma exposure (emotional, physical, and sexual abuse, and emotional and physical neglect). Logistic regression was employed to evaluate salient predictors among the trauma measures for each cluster, personality disorder, and history of attempted suicide and self-harm. All analyses controlled for gender distribution. … CONCLUSION: These results suggest that childhood emotional abuse and neglect are broadly represented among personality disorders, and associated with indices of clinical severity among patients with borderline personality disorder. Childhood sexual and physical abuse are highlighted as predictors of both paranoid and antisocial personality disorders. These results help qualify prior observations of the association of childhood sexual abuse with borderline personality disorder."

[227] Goodman LA, et al., 2001, Recent victimization in women and men with severe mental illness: prevalence and correlates, J Trauma Stress. 2001 Oct;14(4):615-32;

"The problem of violence against individuals with severe mental illness (SMI) has received relatively, little notice, despite several studies suggesting an exceptionally high prevalence of victimization in this population. This paper describes the results of an investigation of the prevalence and correlates of past year physical and sexual assault among a large sample of women and men with SMI drawn from inpatient and outpatient settings across 4 states. Results confirmed preliminary findings of a high prevalence of victimization in this population (with sexual abuse more prevalent for women and physical abuse more prevalent for men), and indicated the existence of a range of correlates of recent victimization, including demographic factors and living circumstances, history of childhood abuse, and psychiatric illness severity and substance abuse."

[228] Briere J, & Elliott DM, 2003, Prevalence and psychological sequelae of self-reported childhood physical and sexual abuse in a general population sample of men and women, Child Abuse Negl. 2003 ct;27(10):1205-22,

"OBJECTIVE: This study examined the prevalence and psychological sequelae of childhood sexual and physical abuse in adults from the general population. METHOD: A national sampling service generated a geographically stratified, random sample of 1,442 subjects from the United States. Subjects were mailed a questionnaire that included the Traumatic Events Survey (TES) [Traumatic Events Survey, Unpublished Psychological Test, Harbor-UCLA Medical Center, Los Angeles] and the Trauma Symptom Inventory (TSI) [Trauma Symptom Inventory Professional Manual, Psychological Assessment Resources, Odessa, FL]. Of all potential subjects, 935 (64.8%) returned substantially completed surveys. … CONCLUSIONS: Childhood sexual and physical abuse is relatively common in the general population, and is associated with a wide variety of psychological symptoms. These relationships remain even after controlling for relevant background variables."

[229] Edwards VJ, et al., 2003, Relationship between multiple forms of childhood maltreatment and adult mental health in community respondents: results from the adverse childhood experiences study, Am J Psychiatry. 2003 Aug;160(8):1453-60,

"OBJECTIVE: This study examined the prevalence of a history of various combinations of childhood maltreatment types (physical abuse, sexual abuse, and witnessing of maternal battering) among adult members of a health maintenance organization (HMO) and explored the relationship with adult mental health of the combinations of types of childhood maltreatment and emotional abuse in the childhood family environment. METHOD: A total of 8,667 adult members of an HMO completed measures of childhood exposure to family dysfunction, which included items on physical and sexual abuse, witnessing of maternal battering, and emotional abuse in the childhood family environment. The adults' current mental health was assessed by using the mental health scale of the Medical Outcomes Study 36-item Short-Form Health Survey. ... CONCLUSIONS: Childhood physical and sexual abuse, as well as witnessing of maternal battering, were common among the adult members of an HMO in this study. Among those reporting any maltreatment, more than one-third had experienced more than one type of maltreatment. A dose-response relation was found between the number of types of maltreatment reported and mental health scores. In addition, an emotionally abusive family environment accentuated the decrements in mental health scores. Future research examining the effects of childhood maltreatment on adult mental health should include assessments of a wide range of abusive experiences, as well as the family atmosphere in which they occur."

[230] Saleptsi E, et al., 2004, Negative and positive childhood experiences across developmental periods in psychiatric patients with different diagnoses - an explorative study, BMC Psychiatry. 2004 Nov 26;4:40,

"BACKGROUND: A high frequency of childhood abuse has often been reported in adult psychiatric patients. The present survey explores the relationship between psychiatric diagnoses and positive and negative life events during childhood and adulthood in psychiatric samples. METHODS: A total of 192 patients with diagnoses of alcohol-related disorders (n = 45), schizophrenic disorders (n = 52), affective disorders (n = 54), and personality disorders (n = 41) completed a 42-item self-rating scale (Traumatic Antecedents Questionnaire, TAQ). The TAQ assesses personal positive experiences (competence and safety) and negative experiences (neglect, separation, secrets, emotional, physical and sexual abuse, trauma witnessing, other traumas, and alcohol and drugs abuse) during four developmental periods, beginning from early childhood to adulthood. Patients were recruited from four Psychiatric hospitals in Germany, Switzerland, and Romania; 63 subjects without any history of mental illness served as controls. ... CONCLUSIONS: The present findings add evidence to the relationship between retrospectively reported childhood experiences and psychiatric diagnoses, and emphasize the fact that a) emotional neglect and abuse are the most prominent negative experiences, b) adolescence is a more 'sensitive' period for negative experiences as compared to early childhood, and c) a high amount of reported emotional and physical abuse occurs in patients with alcohol-related and personality disorders respectively."

[231] Sansone RA, et al., 2005, Childhood trauma and employment disability, Int J Psychiatry Med. 2005;35(4):395-404,

"INTRODUCTION: While the relationship between childhood trauma and employment disability has undergone very limited study, existing data suggest a possible correlation. METHOD: In this study of 91 outpatients in an internal medicine setting, we surveyed participants and inquired about their childhood histories of sexual, physical, and emotional abuse, of physical neglect, and of witnessing violence. We also asked whether participants had ever been on employment disability, either psychiatric or non-psychiatric, and the length of that disability. … CONCLUSIONS: Maltreatment in childhood appears to have a relationship to employment disability in adulthood. The authors discuss the implications of these findings."

[232] Sansone RA, et al., 2006, Childhood trauma, borderline personality symptomatology, and psychophysiological and pain disorders in adulthood, Psychosomatics. 2006 Mar-Apr;47(2):158-62,

"In the empirical literature, there is support for the idea of a relationship between childhood trauma and various psychophysiological as well as pain disorders, and between borderline personality symptomatology and somatic preoccupation, as well as chronic pain. … These [study] data suggest that a general factor associated with various forms of trauma predicts number of psychophysiological and pain disorders and that a specific predictor may be witnessing violence in childhood."

[233] Teicher MH, et al., 2006, Sticks, stones, and hurtful words: relative effects of various forms of childhood maltreatment,

"OBJECTIVE: Childhood maltreatment is an important psychiatric risk factor. Research has focused primarily on the effects of physical abuse, sexual abuse, or witnessing domestic violence. Parental verbal aggression has received little attention as a specific form of abuse. This study was designed to delineate the impact of parental verbal aggression, witnessing domestic violence, physical abuse, and sexual abuse, by themselves and in combination, on psychiatric symptoms. … CONCLUSIONS: Parental verbal aggression was a potent form of maltreatment. Exposure to multiple forms of abuse was associated with very large effect sizes. Most maltreated children had been exposed to multiple types of abuse, and the number of different types is a critically important factor."

[234] McFarlane A, Schrader G, Bookless C, Browne D., 2006, Prevalence of victimization, posttraumatic stress disorder and violent behaviour in the seriously mentally ill, Aust N Z J Psychiatry. 2006 Nov-Dec;40(11-12):1010-5;

"There is evidence that individuals with a mental illness are more likely to report a history of victimization and to be at an increased risk for future victimization" … "A lifetime history of victimization was reported in 87.7% of patients with 46% having lifetime and 32% current PTSD. Most clinicians did not identify the high rates of comorbid PTSD in these patients." … "Victimization may have a negative impact on outcome and may further disadvantage an already vulnerable population.

declaring them appropriate targets for special laws, extra-legal deprivations of civil

liberties, and whatever abuse and humiliation psychiatrists and their institutions might

dish out as "treatment modalities" [236] [237] [238] [239] ;

These findings have both clinical and policy implications for the long-term management of people with
mental illness."

[235] Teplin LA, McClelland GM, Abram KM, Weiner DA, Crime victimization in adults with severe mental
illness: comparison with the National Crime Victimization Survey, Arch Gen Psychiatry. 2005
Aug;62(8):911-21;

"Sixteen agencies providing outpatient, day, and residential treatment to persons with SMI in
Chicago, Ill ... Randomly selected, stratified sample of 936 patients aged 18 or older (483 men, 453
women) ... The comparison group comprised 32,449 participants in the National Crime Victimization
Survey ... RESULTS: More than one quarter of persons with SMI had been victims of a violent crime in
the past year, a rate more than 11 times higher than the general population rates even after controlling for
demographic differences between the 2 samples (P<.001). The annual incidence of violent crime in the
SMI sample (168.2 incidents per 1000 persons) is more than 4 times higher than the general population
rates (39.9 incidents per 1000 persons) (P<.001). Depending on the type of violent crime (rape/sexual
assault, robbery, assault, and their subcategories), prevalence was 6 to 23 times greater among persons
with SMI than among the general population."

[236] O'Connor v. Donaldson, 422 U.S. 563 (1975),

"O'Connor described Donaldson's treatment as "milieu therapy." But witnesses from the hospital staff
conceded that, in the context of this case, "milieu therapy" was a euphemism for confinement in the
"milieu" of a mental hospital. For substantial periods, Donaldson was simply kept in a large room that
housed 60 patients, many of whom were under criminal commitment."

[237] Sileo, Chi Chi, 1994, Rip-off depress mental health care – fraud in psychiatric hospital practices,
Insight on the News, Jan 24, 1994, citing a woman lured and forced into psychiatric commitment by an
abusive, insurance-scamming hospital falsely posing as a fat reduction spa, among other examples.

[238] Deneen, Sally, 1988, Complaints about psychiatric hospitals rise, August 19, 1988, Sun- Sentinel,
Florida,

"Complaining they were milked of insurance money or given too much medication, a growing number
of residents has filed complaints against Lake and Fair Oaks psychiatric hospitals -- making Palm Beach
County No. 1 in the state in allegations against private treatment centers."

q-   Further abused those already traumatized by mere circumstance[240] [241] [242], such as

accident and exposure to environmental hazards;

---

[239] Electric Shocks Are Inhumane And Barbaric, http://www.cchrflorida.org/blog/electric-shocks-areinhumane-and-barbaric/ and http://www.youtube.com/watch?v=RlJ10qnrfl4&

[240] McNally, RJ, et al., 2003, Does early psychological intervention promote recovery from posttraumatic stress?, *Psychological Science in the Public Interest,* vol. 4, no. 2, November 2003, pp. 45-79, notes in Table 3 the high correlations of having both acute stress disorder and post-traumatic stress disorder in victims of burns, brain injury, motor vehicle accidents and cancer;

"The single most important indicator of subsequent risk for chronic PTSD appears to be the severity or number of posttrauma symptoms from about 1 to 2 weeks after the event onward (provided that the event is over and that there is no ongoing threat)."; notes in Table 3 the high correlations of having both acute stress disorder and post-traumatic stress disorder in victims of burns, brain injury, motor vehicle accidents and cancer;

"Current research indicates that the single most important indicator for the risk of chronic PTSD is the severity of PTSD symptoms." …

" Another indicator relevant to early identification of people who will develop chronic PTSD is depression. In one study, survivors who had major depression in addition to PTSD at 1 month after the event showed greater decreases in their ability to function at work and with friends and family and had a greater chance of having PTSD at 4 months than did those who had PTSD without depression (e.g., Shalev, Freedman, et al., 1998)."

"There are important reasons for screening trauma survivors before providing an intervention. First, one has to bear in mind that traumatic events can trigger not only PTSD, but also a range of other disorders, such as psychosis." …

"The way trauma survivors interpret the initial posttrauma symptoms, such as reexperiencing, numbness, and irritability, predicts the persistence of symptoms independently of symptom severity (Dunmore et al., 2001; Ehlers et al., 1998). Survivors who interpret these symptoms as signs that they might be going crazy, about to lose control, or permanently changed for the worse are at greater risk for chronic symptoms and in greater need of treatment than are those who interpret their symptoms as a normal part of recovery. Sadly, many trauma survivors endure long-lasting physical consequences, such as chronic pain, visible scars, or loss of limbs. These survivors have a greater chance of having chronic PTSD and thus a greater need for help than those who are unhurt or who recover well from their physical injuries (Blanchard et al., 1997; Ehlers et al., 1998)."

r- Forced people vulnerable to self-incrimination [243] [244] to do so under psychiatric

evaluation without benefit of counsel [245], leaving evaluators unfettered in making the

---

[241] Medical Encyclopedia: Post-traumatic stress disorder,

http://www.lnlmnih.gov/medlineplus/print/ency/article/000925.htm, notes that PTSD can cause repeated

reliving of events, flashbacks, nightmares, a sense of having no future, marked mood changes, irritability,

outbursts of anger, sleeping difficulties, difficulty concentrating, hypervigilance, loss of interest in normal

activities, anxiety, stress, tension, depression, phobias, and alcohol and substance abuse.

[242] Kilburn, KH and JC Thornton, 1995, Protracted Neurotoxicity from Chlordane Sprayed to Kill

Termites, Environmental Health Perspectives, Volume 103, Number 7-8, July-August 1995, pp. 690-94,

compared 216 adults exposed to Chlordane inside apartments due to it sprayed on the outside wooden

surfaces, compared to 174 non-exposed adults. Tables 1 & 2 show that exposed adults had significantly

higher rates of tension, depression, anger, fatigue and confusion, as well as slower reaction times, worse

balance.

"Chlordane exposure was associated with protracted impairment of neurophysiological and

psychological functions. The central nervous system is the most important target of chlorinated

cyclodiene insecticides. Human exposure should be prohibited."

[243] Turgeon, Carolyn, Jan 2005, Interview: Stephen V. Manley, Judge, Mental Health Treatment Court,

Santa Clara County, California; http://www.courtinnovation.org/research/stephen-v-manley-judge-mental-

healthtreatment-court-santa-clara-county-california;

"I do not believe that just any judge could walk in and preside over a mental health court. A judge

has to be committed, very patient, and willing to accept criticism from clients. Because mentally ill

people are very honest. They will tell you almost everything and they will tell you what is and isn't

working and what they want—if you ever bother to listen to them."

[244] Roberson, Shawn. 2009. Interrogations and False Confessions – What Attorneys Should Know From

the Social Sciences. The Gauntlet, Law Journal of the Oklahoma Criminal Defense Lawyers Association,

Spring 2009:57-71;

"This article will outline how social science research during the past several decades supports the

conclusions that: 1) false confessions do occur; 2) confession evidence is the most damning of all forms

of evidence; 3) most suspects waive *Miranda*, especially innocent suspects; 4) law enforcement

investigators have been widely trained to believe in techniques of "lie detection" that are not empirically

supported; 5) law enforcement investigators have been widely trained in psychological methods of

interrogating suspects which raise the risk an innocent person will confess; 6) jurors are likely influenced

worst possible interpretations of their statements, to the financial and professional

benefit of evaluators and their institutions[246];

s-   Caused unequal treatment under the law on the basis of medical conditions which

are virtually indistinguishable from each other in their effect upon behavior [247] [248] [249]

---

by coerced confessions, even when they view them as coerced and they are instructed to ignore them; and 7) certain groups are at risk for interrogative suggestibility (*e.g.*, minors, persons with mental illness, intoxicated persons, *etc.*).”

[245] Estelle v. Smith, 451 U.S. 454 (1981)

“This is by no means to say that respondent had any right to have his counsel present at any examination. In this regard I join the Court's careful delimiting of the Sixth Amendment issue, *ante,* at 470, n. 14.”

“Rather, the issue before **us** is whether a defendant's Sixth Amendment right to the assistance of counsel is abridged when the defendant is not given prior opportunity to consult with counsel about his participation in the psychiatric examination. But cf. n. 15, *infra.* Respondent does not assert, and the Court of Appeals did not find, any constitutional right to have counsel actually present during the examination. In fact, the Court of Appeals recognized that "an attorney present during the psychiatric interview could contribute little and might seriously disrupt the examination." 602 F. 2d, at 708. Cf. *Thornton* v. *Corcoran,* 132 **U. S.** App. D. C. 232, 242, 248, 407 F. 2d 695, 705, 711 (1969) (opinion concurring in part and dissenting in part).”

[Which has extended from criminal to civil commitment cases in practice]

[246] Miller, Sarah L. and Stanley L. Brodsky, 2011, Risky Business: Addressing the Consequences of Predicting Violence, J Am Acad Psychiatry Law 39:396–401, 2011, also noting (p 397) that psychiatric evaluators have more to fear from releasing a violent patient, which garners significant publicity, than would falsely holding a non-violent patient, often done secretly under alleged HIPPA guidelines, even if such evaluators are overconfident of their abilities: “In one prospective study, clinicians were generally confident in their risk assessments, although some findings suggest that higher levels of confidence were associated with lower accuracy in predicting future aggression.22”

[247] Antonius D, 2014, Behavioral health symptoms associated with chronic traumatic encephalopathy: a critical review of the literature and recommendations for treatment and research, J Neuropsychiatry Clin Neurosci. 2014 Fall;26(4):313-22, “Chronic traumatic encephalopathy (CTE) is a neurodegenerative syndrome that has been linked to serious psychiatric symptoms, including depression, aggression, and suicidal behavior.”

250 251 252 253 254 255 256 257 258 259 260 261 262 263 264 265 266 267 268; for example, Oklahoma

[248] Baguley, IJ, 2006, Aggressive behavior following brain injury: How common is common?, J Head Trauma Rehabil, 2006, Jan-Feb, 21(1):45-46, "Aggression is a common, fluctuating, and long-term problem following TBI."

[249] Bay, E et al., 2004, Chronic stress conditions do explain posttraumatic brain injury depression, Res Theory Nurs Pract, 2004 Summer-Fall, 18(2-3);213-28, "These findings support stress-diathesis theory within the psychiatric literature and a linkage between chronic stress, an indicator of allostatic load, and post-TBI depression."

[250] Bay, E & Donders, J, 2008, Risk factors for depressive symptoms after mild-to-moderate traumatic brain injury, Brain Inj, Mar 2008, 22(3):233-41, "Perceived stress, one indicator of allostatic load, explains a considerable amount of the variance in depressive symptoms after mild-moderate TBI."

[251] Bogner J, Pilot study of traumatic brain injury and alcohol misuse among service members, Brain Inj. 2015, 29(7-8):905-14

[252] DeKosky, ST, 2013, Acute and chronic traumatic encephalopathies: pathogenesis and biomarkers, Nat Rev Neurol. 2013 Apr;9(4):192-200,

"the entity of chronic traumatic encephalopathy (CTE)--which is marked by prominent neuropsychiatric features including dementia, parkinsonism, depression, agitation, psychosis, and aggression--has become increasingly recognized as a potential late outcome of repetitive TBI ... Seemingly mild 'closed-head' TBI, in which the skull is not fractured, can lead to diverse and sometimes disabling symptoms such as chronic headaches, dizziness and vertigo, difficulty in concentrating, word-finding problems, depression, irritability and impulsiveness. The duration of such symptoms is variable, but can be months or longer. Post-traumatic stress disorder (PTSD) is a frequent accompaniment of military-related TBI, especially severe cases.5–14 ... Severe single-incident TBI, with or without skull fracture, can lead to permanent brain damage, with incomplete recovery and residual sensory, motor and cognitive deficits. Unlike mild repetitive TBI, discussed below, severe single-incident TBI is associated with increased risk of late-onset Alzheimer disease (AD).15–20 ... At least 12 former National Football League players have committed suicide over the past 25 years, many suffering from cognitive and affective symptoms. In two of the more recent suicides, the players shot themselves in the heart, which enabled their brains to be studied postmortem.53,55,56"

[253] Draper, K, et al., 2007, Psychosocial and emotional outcomes 10 years following traumatic brain injury, J Head Trauma Rehabil, Sept 2007, 22(5):278-87, "Posttraumatic amnesia duration was most strongly associated with psychosocial outcome measured by relatives; anxiety, aggression, and depression

were the strongest predictors when ratings were assigned by participants with TBI. Self-reported fatigue, depression and alcohol use were the strongest predictors of aggression."

[254] Hoge, CW, 2008, Mild traumatic brain injury in U.S. Soldiers returning from Iraq, N Engl J Med, Jan 2008, 358(5):453-63, "Mild traumatic brain injury (i.e., concussion) occurring among soldiers deployed in Iraq is strongly associated with PTSD and physical health problems 3 to 4 months after the soldiers return home. PTSD and depression are important mediators of the relationship between mild traumatic brain injury and physical health problems."

[255] Ilie, G, et al., Suicidality, bullying and other conduct and mental health correlates of traumatic brain injury in adolescents, PLoS One. 2014 Apr 15;9(4),

"Lifetime TBI was defined as head injury that resulted in being unconscious for at least 5 minutes or being retained in the hospital for at least one night, and was reported by 19.5% (95%CI:17.3,21.9) of students. When holding constant sex, grade, and complex sample design, students with TBI had significantly greater odds of reporting elevated psychological distress (AOR = 1.52), attempting suicide (AOR = 3.39), seeking counselling through a crisis help-line (AOR = 2.10), and being prescribed medication for anxiety, depression, or both (AOR = 2.45). Moreover, students with TBI had higher odds of being victimized through bullying at school (AOR = 1.70), being cyber-bullied (AOR = 2.05), and being threatened with a weapon at school (AOR = 2.90), compared with students who did not report TBI. Students with TBI also had higher odds of victimizing others and engaging in numerous violent as well as nonviolent conduct behaviours."

[256] Jorge RE, 2015, Mood disorders, Handb Clin Neurol. 2015;128:613-31,

"Mood disturbances, especially depressive disorders, are the most frequent neuropsychiatric complication of traumatic brain injury (TBI). These disorders have a complex clinical presentation and are highly comorbid with anxiety, substance misuse, and other behavioral alterations such as impulsivity and aggression. Furthermore, once developed, mood disorders tend to have a chronic and refractory course. Thus, the functional repercussion of these disorders is huge, affecting the rehabilitation process and the long-term outcome of TBI patients."

[257] Kaufer DI, 2015, Neurobehavioral assessment, Continuum (Minneap Minn). 2015 Jun;21(3 Behavioral Neurology and Neuropsychiatry):597-612,

"Recent Findings: Behavioral neurology and neuropsychiatry has grown as a subspecialty along with increased recognition of two common brain disorders: dementia and traumatic brain injury. Alzheimer disease is a highly prevalent dementia and a prototypical memory disorder, which has led to a primary focus on cognitive screening and assessment. By contrast, recent attention concerning possible long-term sequelae of repetitive traumatic brain injury has emphasized aberrant behavior (eg, depression, impulsivity, aggression)."

[258] Laskowski, RA, et al., Chapter 4 Pathophysiology of Mild TBI Implications for Altered Signaling Pathways, Kobeissy FH, editor. Brain Neurotrauma: Molecular, Neuropsychological, and Rehabilitation Aspects. Boca Raton (FL): CRC Press/Taylor & Francis; 2015,

" Moderate to severe TBI is a major cause of injury-induced death and disability with an annual incidence of approximately 500 in 100,000 people affected in the United States (Sosin et al., 1989; Kraus and McArthur, 1996; Rutland-Brown et al., 2006). However, approximately 80% of all TBI cases are categorized as mild head injuries (Bazarian et al., 2005; Langlois et al., 2006). It is important to note that these approximations are underestimates because they do not account for incidents of TBI in which the person does not seek medical care (Faul et al., 2010). Recent estimates to correct for this underreporting have placed the annual incidence at approximately 3.8 million (Bazarian et al., 2005; Ropper and Gorson, 2007; Halstead and Walter, 2010). …

"Behavioral manifestations after TBI include personality changes, depression, and anxiety. Personality changes describe aggression, impulsivity, irritability, emotional lability, and apathy. Major depression is one of the most frequently reported behavioral sequelae of TBI, accounting for approximately 25% to 40% of cases of moderate-to-severe TBI (Riggio and Wong, 2009)."

[259] McKee AC, 2013, The spectrum of disease in chronic traumatic encephalopathy, Brain. 2013 Jan;136(Pt 1):43-64,

"Symptoms in stage I chronic traumatic encephalopathy included headache and loss of attention and concentration. Additional symptoms in stage II included depression, explosivity and short-term memory loss. In stage III, executive dysfunction and cognitive impairment were found, and in stage IV, dementia, word-finding difficulty and aggression were characteristic."

[260] Moore RD, 2015, Neurophysiological correlates of persistent psycho-affective alterations in athletes with a history of concussion, Brain Imaging Behav. 2015 Nov 5. [Epub ahead of print], "The current study suggests that athletes with a history of concussion who made a complete return to play and reported to be asymptomatic on a commonly used symptom checklist may still exhibit neural activity associated with increased levels of depression, anxiety and anger/hostility."

[261] Seel RT, 2003, Depression after traumatic brain injury, Arch Phys Med Rehabil, Feb 2003, 84(2):177-84, "Patients with TBI are at great reisk of developing depressive symptoms."

[262] Stéfan A, 2016, What are the disruptive symptoms of behavioral disorders after traumatic brain injury? A systematic review leading to recommendations for good practices, Ann Phys Rehabil Med. 2016 Jan 4, [Epub ahead of print],

"Systematic review of the literature targeting epidemiological data related to behavioral disorders after traumatic brain injury … Two hundred and ninety-nine articles were identified. The responsibility of traumatic brain injury (TBI) in the onset of behavioral disorders is unequivocal. Globally, behavioral disorders are twice more frequent after TBI than orthopedic trauma without TBI (Masson et al., 1996). These disorders are classified into disruptive primary behaviors by excess (agitation 11-70%, aggression 25-39%, irritability 29-71%, alcohol abuse 7-26% drug abuse 2-20%), disruptive primary behaviors by default (apathy 20-71%), affective disorders - anxiety - psychosis (depression 12-76%, anxiety 0.8-24,5%, posttraumatic stress 11-18%, obsessive-compulsive disorders 1.2-30%, psychosis 0.7%), suicide attempts and suicide 1%."

[263] Stein TD, 2014, Chronic traumatic encephalopathy: a spectrum of neuropathological changes following repetitive brain trauma in athletes and military personnel, Alzheimers Res Ther. 2014 Jan 15;6(1):4

"Chronic traumatic encephalopathy (CTE) is a progressive neurodegenerative disease that occurs in association with repetitive traumatic brain injury experienced in sport and military service. In most instances, the clinical symptoms of the disease begin after a long period of latency ranging from several years to several decades. The initial symptoms are typically insidious, consisting of irritability, impulsivity, aggression, depression, short-term memory loss and heightened suicidality. The symptoms progress slowly over decades to include cognitive deficits and dementia."

[264] Sundman M, et al., 2015, Neuroimaging assessment of early and late neurobiological sequelae of traumatic brain injury: implications for CTE, Front Neurosci. 2015 Sep 24(9):334,

"Recent evidence indicates that the resultant chronic neurobiological sequelae following head trauma may, at least in part, contribute to a pathologically distinct disease known as Chronic Traumatic Encephalopathy (CTE). The clinical manifestation of CTE is variable, but the symptoms of this progressive disease include impaired memory and cognition, affective disorders (i.e., impulsivity, aggression, depression, suicidality, etc.), and diminished motor control."

[265] Vanderploeg, RD, 2007, Long-term morbidities following self-reported mild traumatic brain injury, J Clin Exp Neuropsychol. 2007 Aug, 29(6):585-98.

[266] Weyer JC, 2013, Pain and mild traumatic brain injury: the implications of pain severity on emotional and cognitive functioning, Brain Inj. 2013;27(10):1134-40, "however, the high pain group had significantly more emotional residuals; particularly elevated on the RNBI were the Anger and Aggression, Anxiety, Depression and Paranoia and Suspicion sub-scales."

[267] Wong GK, 2014, Neuropsychiatric disturbance after aneurysmal subarachnoid hemorrhage, J Clin Neurosci. 2014 Oct;21(10):1695-8,

"Although aneurysmal subarachnoid hemorrhage (aSAH) accounts for only 3-5% of all strokes, a high degree of morbidity has been reported in this relatively young subset of patients. Neuropsychiatric disturbance has often been neglected in these reports. ... One hundred and three aSAH patients' spouses

State Mental Health Code, Title 43A[269], states that in the absence of risk of harm to self or others due to mental illness or drug or alcohol use, a "person requiring treatment" shall not include a person impaired by age, dementia, Alzheimer's disease, mental retardation, developmental disabilities, seizure disorder [270], traumatic brain injury or homelessness, so that "risk of harm" due to these conditions does not "require treatment", i.e., involuntary civil commitment;

This Court's blind eye

87. Because when this Court can or should see that matters of constitutional justice are

clearly involved in a case before it, it does this Court no honor or respect, sets no

good example, and does this society no justice, for this Court either to turn a blind eye

---

or caregivers completed the CNPI. Forty-two (41%) patients were reported to have one or more domain(s) of neuropsychiatric disturbance. Common neuropsychiatric disturbance domains included agitation/aggression, depression, apathy/indifference, irritability/lability, and appetite/eating disturbance. Chronic neuropsychiatric disturbance was associated with presence of chronic hydrocephalus."

[268] Kilburn, KH and JC Thornton, 1995, Protracted Neurotoxicity from Chlordane Sprayed to Kill Termites, Environmental Health Perspectives, Volume 103, Number 7-8, July-August 1995, pp. 690-94, Tables 1 & 2 show that exposed adults had significantly higher rates of tension, depression, anger, fatigue and confusion, as well as slower reaction times, worse balance.

[269] OSC 43A-1-103.13

[270] Kirby, ML, et al., 2001, Neurotoxicity of the organochlorine insecticide heptachlor to murine striatal dopamainergic pathways, Toxicological Sciences, 61:100-106, states that

"These results suggest that heptachlor, and perhaps other organochlorine insecticides, exert selective effects on striatal dopaminergic neurons and may play a role in the eitiology of idiopathic Parkinson's disease." [Combined with Kilburn & Thornton, 1995, suggest that where the same pesticide may produce both psychiatric and neurological disturbances, Oklahoma law punishes or circumscribes liberties in one but not the other, as in Skinner v. Oklahoma (1942)]

to them because they were not fully expressed by petitioners [271] [272] [273] [274] [275] [276] [277]; or to uphold the common prejudices or junk science of the day [278] [279] [280] [281] [282] [283]; or to

---

[271] In re Gault - 387 U.S. 1 (1967), "The petition for habeas corpus did not raise the Fifth Amendment issue, nor did any of the witnesses focus on it."

[272] Rogers v. Okin, 738 F2d 1 (1984), "Defendants did not present the seclusion issue to the Supreme Court. Mills v. Rogers, 457 U.S. at 294"

[273] United States v. Georgia et al, no. 04-1203 (2006),

"From the many allegations in Goodman's pro se complaint and his subsequent filings in the District Court, it is not clear precisely what conduct he intended to allege in support of his Title II claims. Because the Eleventh Circuit did not address the issue, it is likewise unclear to what extent the conduct underlying Goodman's constitutional claims also violated Title II. Moreover, the Eleventh Circuit ordered that the suit be remanded to the District Court to permit Goodman to amend his complaint, but instructed him to revise his factual allegations to exclude his "frivolous" claims--some of which are quite far afield from actual constitutional violations (under either the Eighth Amendment or some other constitutional provision), or even from Title II violations. See, e.g., App. 50 (demanding a "steam table" for Goodman's housing unit). It is therefore unclear whether Goodman's amended complaint will assert Title II claims premised on conduct that does not independently violate the Fourteenth Amendment. Once Goodman's complaint is amended, the lower courts will be best situated to determine in the first instance, on a claim-by- claim basis, (1) which aspects of the State's alleged conduct violated Title II; (2) to what extent such misconduct also violated the Fourteenth Amendment; and (3) insofar as such misconduct violated Title II but did not violate the Fourteenth Amendment, whether Congress's purported abrogation of sovereign immunity as to that class of conduct is nevertheless valid." [Pro Se petitioners rarely have the legal experience to separate wheat from chaff, or the resources to hire those who can, and thus loose the majority of their cases – an extremely disparate outcome which this Court has never adequately addressed.]

[274] WHITNEY v. CALIFORNIA, 274 U.S. 357 (1927),

"She might have required that the issue be determined either by the court or the jury. She claimed below that the statute as applied to her violated the Federal Constitution; but she did not claim that it was void because there was no clear and present danger of serious evil, nor did she request that the existence of these conditions of a valid measure thus restricting the rights of free speech and assembly be passed upon by the court or a jury."

[275] Buck v. Bell, 274 U.S. 200 (1927),

History shows that Buck's lawyer was a proponent for sterilization, chosen by the other side, who presented no expert witnesses on her behalf, and raised no objections either to the validity of eugenics, or to the expert witnesses appearing against her, or to the hypothetical questions or hearsay raised against her. Furthermore, none of the Judges in the case, up to and including the U.S. Supreme Court, bothered the check the actual school records of either Carrie Buck or her daughter Vivian, which would have destroyed the contention of "three generations of imbeciles". This case of railroading was and remains a shameful blot on this Court's integrity.

[276] Jacobson v. Massachusetts - 197 U.S. 11 (1905),

"The legislature assumed that some children, by reason of their condition at the time, might not be fit subjects of vaccination, and it is suggested -- and we will not say without reason -- that such is the case with some adults. But the defendant did not offer to prove that, by reason of his then condition, he was, in fact, not a fit subject of vaccination at the time he was informed of the requirement of the regulation adopted by the Board of Health. It is entirely consistent with his offer of proof that, after reaching full age, he had become, so far as medical skill could discover, and, when informed of the regulation of the Board of Health, was, a fit subject of vaccination, and that the vaccine matter to be used in his case was such as any medical practitioner of good standing would regard as proper to be used."

[277] Heller v. Doe, 509 U. S. 312 (1993),

"Respondents' claim that the statutes should be reviewed under a heightened scrutiny standard is not properly presented, since it was not raised below and the lower courts ruled only on the ground of rationalbasis review. Pp. 318-319."

[278] Scott v. Sanford, 60 U.S. 393 (1856),

"On the contrary, they were at that time considered as a subordinate [Page 60 U. S. 405] and inferior class of beings who had been subjugated by the dominant race, and, whether emancipated or not, yet remained subject to their authority, and had no rights or privileges but such as those who held the power and the Government might choose to grant them." …

"They had for more than a century before been regarded as beings of an inferior order, and altogether unfit to associate with the white race either in social or political relations, and so far inferior that they had no rights which the white man was bound to respect, and that the negro might justly and lawfully be reduced to slavery for his benefit. He was bought and sold, and treated as an ordinary article of merchandise and traffic whenever a profit could be made by it. This opinion was at that time fixed and universal in the civilized portion of the white race. It was regarded as an axiom in morals as well as in politics which no one thought of disputing or supposed to be open to dispute, and men in every grade and position in society daily and habitually acted upon it in their private pursuits, as well as in matters of public concern, without doubting for a moment the correctness of this opinion." …

"They have continued to treat them as an inferior class, and to subject them to strict police regulations, drawing a broad line of distinction between the citizen and the slave races, and legislating in relation to them upon the same principle which prevailed at the time of the Declaration of Independence. As relates to these States, it is too plain for argument that they have never been regarded as a part of the people or citizens of the State, nor supposed to possess any political rights which the dominant race might not withhold or grant at their pleasure." … ad nauseum.

[279] Plessy v. Ferguson, 163 U.S. 537 (1896),

"So, too, in the *Civil Rights Cases,* 109 U.S. 3, 24, it was said that the act of a mere individual, the owner of an inn, a public conveyance or place of amusement, refusing accommodations to colored people cannot be justly regarded as imposing any badge of slavery or servitude upon the applicant,"

"It is claimed by the plaintiff in error that, in any mixed community, the reputation of belonging to the dominant race, in this instance the white race, is property in the same sense that a right of action or of inheritance is property. Conceding this to be so for the purposes of this case, we are unable to see how this statute deprives him of, or in any way affects his right to, such property. If he be a white man and assigned to a colored coach, he may have his action for damages against the company for being deprived of his so-called property. Upon the other hand, if he be a colored man and be so assigned, he has been deprived of no property, **since he is not lawfully entitled to the reputation of being a white man.** [emphasis added]"

"The object of the amendment was undoubtedly to enforce the absolute equality of the two races before the law, but, in the nature of things, it could not have been intended to abolish distinctions based upon color, or to enforce social, as distinguished from political, equality, or a commingling of the two races upon terms unsatisfactory to either. Laws permitting, and even requiring, their separation in places where they are liable to be brought into contact do not necessarily imply the inferiority of either race to the other, and have been generally, if not universally, recognized as within the competency of the state legislatures in the exercise of their police power. The most common instance of this is connected with the establishment of separate schools for white and colored children, which has been held to be a valid exercise of the legislative power even by courts of States where the political rights of the colored race have been longest and most earnestly enforced." …

"We consider the underlying fallacy of the plaintiff's argument to consist in the assumption that the enforced separation of the two races stamps the colored race with a badge of inferiority. If this be so, it is not by reason of anything found in the act, but solely because the colored race chooses to put that construction upon it. … The argument also assumes that social prejudices may be overcome by legislation, and that equal rights cannot be secured to the negro except by an enforced commingling of the two races. We cannot accept this proposition. If the two races are to meet upon terms of social equality, it must be the result of natural affinities, a mutual appreciation of each other's merits, and a voluntary consent of individuals. As was said by the Court of Appeals of New York in *People v. Gallagher,* 93 N. Y. 438, 448, … Legislation is powerless to eradicate racial instincts or to abolish distinctions based upon physical differences, and the attempt to do so can only result in accentuating the difficulties of the present situation. If the civil and political rights of both races be equal, one cannot be inferior to the other civilly [p552] or politically. If one race be inferior to the other socially, the Constitution of the United States cannot put them upon the same plane."

[280] Gould v. Gould, Supp Ct of Conn (1905), although in a Connecticut State court, never struck down by this Court, wherein the Connecticut court wrote, demonstrating "equal treatment under the law",

"That epilepsy is a disease of a peculiarly serious and revolting character, tending to weaken mental force, and often descending from parent to child, or entailing upon the offspring of the sufferer some other grave form of nervous malady, is a matter of common knowledge, of which courts will take judicial notice. State v. Main, 69 Conn. 123, 135. One mode of guarding against the perpetuation of epilepsy obviously is to forbid sexual intercourse with those afflicted by it, and to preclude such opportunities for sexual intercourse as marriage furnishes. To impose such a restriction upon the right to contract marriage, if not intrinsically unreasonable, is no invasion of the equality of all men before the law, if it applies equally to all under the same circumstances who belong to a certain class of persons, which class can reasonably be regarded as one requiring special legislation either for their protection or for the protection from them of the community at large. It cannot be pronounced by the judiciary to be intrinsically unreasonable, if it should be regarded as a determination by the General Assembly that a law of this kind is necessary for the preservation of public health, and if there are substantial grounds for believing that such determination is supported by the facts upon which it is apparent that it was based. Holden v. Hardy, 169 U.S. 366, 398; Bissell v. Davison, 65 Conn. 183, 192. There can be no doubt *245245 as to the opinion of the General Assembly, nor as to its resting on substantial foundations. The class of persons to whom the statute applies is not one arbitrarily formed to suit its purpose. It is certain and definite. It is a class capable of endangering the health of families and adding greatly to the sum of human suffering. Between the members of this class there is no discrimination, and the prohibitions of the statute cease to operate when, by the attainment of a certain age by one of those whom it affects, the occasion for the restriction is deemed to become less imperative."

[Note the use of the words "revolting" and "weaken mental force" to justify requiring "the protection from them [epileptics] of the community at large", and "for their protection" to justify forbidding epileptics for marry according to the Third Principle, for their own alleged benefit. Note the justification of applying such deprivations to epileptics as a class by the claim of applying it equally to all epileptics, regardless of the source of their epilepsy, whether due to non-inheritable brain trauma from physical or environmental trauma, or actual genetic inheritance (if even possible). Thus the ignorance of the time justified judicial bigotry, as it does today with mental illness.]

[281] Buck v. Bell - 274 U.S. 200 (1927),

"Carrie Buck is a feeble minded white woman who was committed to the State Colony above mentioned in due form. She is the daughter of a feeble minded mother in the same institution, and the mother of an illegitimate feeble minded child." ...

"the Commonwealth is supporting in various institutions many defective persons who, if now discharged, would become [Page 274 U. S. 206] a menace, but, if incapable of procreating, might be discharged with safety and become self-supporting with benefit to themselves and to society, and that experience has shown that heredity plays an important part in the transmission of insanity, imbecility, &c." ...

"It would be strange if it could not call upon those who already sap the strength of the State for these lesser sacrifices, often not felt to be such by those concerned, in order to prevent our being swamped with incompetence. It is better for all the world if, instead of waiting to execute degenerate offspring for crime or to let them starve for their imbecility, society can prevent those who are manifestly unfit from continuing their kind. The principle that sustains compulsory vaccination is broad enough to cover cutting the Fallopian tubes. *Jacobson v. Massachusetts,* 197 U. S. 11. **Three generations of imbeciles are enough.** [emphasis added]"

[282] Pfeiffer, David, 1994, Eugenics and Disability Discrimination, Disability & Society, 9 (4), 1994, pages 481- 99, connects the current attitudes towards people with disabilities to Buck v. Bell (1927), the eugenics movement, and the attitudes and rulings of this Court,

"The Court struck down a state statute which prohibited interracial marriage as a violation of these principles in Loving v. Virginia, 388 U.S. 1 (1967). However, the Court never struck down a state statute which limited marriage by or to a disabled person even when equal protection was clearly violated." ...

"Physicians and hospital administrators routinely allow newly born disabled infants to die. They disconnect the life sustaining apparatus of elderly persons because their quality of life is too meager. Parents who discover that the mother is carrying a "defective" fetus are counselled to obtain an abortion. (Miringoff, 1989, 1991) Wolfensberger (cited in Herr, 1984: 8) estimates that some 200,000 abortions a year are for this reason.

"Disabled children who are allowed to live receive second-rate or worse education in public schools. Some disabled children, especially if the child has AIDS, receive no education at all. Disabled people today are fired or not hired in the first place because of their disability. …

"In a number of states former residents in state schools and hospitals are reinstitutionalized because there is not sufficient funds appropriated for community centers. Public housing is constructed to be not accessible and tenants who behave in a peculiar way are evicted. Citizens with hearing and vision impairments are denied access to public documents. Other disabled persons who are judged not able to manage daily tasks are sterilized for their own "benefit." They are also prohibited from marrying or from parenting their own children.

"Disabled persons are also the outcasts of academia. It was public attitudes which allowed the oppressive laws to be promulgated and implemented, but it was academia which gave justification for those laws. (Hahn, 1985b; Allen, 1986; Weiss, 1987; Gelb, 1989; Meile, Shanks-Meile, & Spurgin, 1989; Nelkin & Tancredi, 1989; Weingart, 1989; Mazumdar, 1992; Blackford, 1993)"

[283] Heller v. Doe, 509 U. S. 312 (1993),

"In contrast, since manifestations of mental illness may be sudden, past behavior may not be an adequate predictor of future actions. A higher standard for the mentally ill is also justified on the ground that, in general, their treatment is much more intrusive than that received by the mentally retarded."

[Having cited Monahan's work, The Clinical Prediction of Violent Behavior, ten years before in Barefoot (1983), this Court has reason to know this is false, that violent behavior in people with mental illness is limited to a small minority with prior and repetitive histories of violence, as well as drug and alcohol abuse. Thus this Court succumbs to the bigotry of the day, to justify "treatment" of a "much more intrusive" character.]

"Rather than increasing the risk of an erroneous deprivation, allowing close relatives and guardians to participate as parties actually increases a proceeding's accuracy by putting valuable information before the court. It also implements the State's interest in providing family members a voice in such proceedings."

[While family members should have a voice, this does not guarantee that such voices are unbiased and due process is thereby preserved. In Buck v. Bell (1927), there is strong suspicion that Carrie Buck's foster family argued for commitment over the embarrassment of one of their family raping and impregnating Ms. Buck. In the psychiatric hospital insurance scams of the 1980s-90s, heavy commercial advertising convinced many families to commit their mentally healthy and harmless teenagers for simple teenage rebellion. (see other references herein)]

imagine and Decide how others must live [284], without any reference to sociological or

other scientific research[285], or without any question to those whose lives this Court

imagines, or humane consideration of the impacts [286]; .

---

[284] Toyota v. Williams, 534 U.S. 184, 202 (2002), in which this Court elevated a Japanese cultural value, that everyone should work hard enough to be able to do everything that everyone else can [Alix Spiegel, November 12, 2012 4:00 AM, Struggle For Smarts? How Eastern And Western Cultures Tackle Learning, NPR Morning Edition, http://www.npr.org/blogs/health/2012/11/12/164793058/struggle...] into a somewhat perverse "business necessity" under the terms of the Americans with Disabilities Act, when accommodating Williams to allow her to do what work she could was both simple and expedient.

"*Held:* The Sixth Circuit did not apply the proper standard in determining that respondent was disabled under the ADA because it analyzed only a limited class of manual tasks and failed to ask whether respondent's impairments prevented or restricted her from performing tasks that are of central importance to most people's daily lives. Pp. 7—18." …. **[Contrary to this Court's Opinion, proud and productive work is "of central importance to most people's daily lives".]**

"Even more critically, the manual tasks unique to any particular job are not necessarily important parts of most people's lives. As a result, occupation-specific tasks may have only limited relevance to the manual task inquiry. In this case, "repetitive work with hands and arms extended at or above shoulder levels for extended periods of time," 224 F.3d, at 843, the manual task on which the Court of Appeals relied, is not an important part of most people's daily lives. The court, therefore, should not have considered respondent's inability to do such manual work in her specialized assembly line job as sufficient proof that she was substantially limited in performing manual tasks.

"At the same time, the Court of Appeals appears to have disregarded the very type of evidence that it should have focused upon. It treated as irrelevant "[t]he fact that [respondent] can … ten[d] to her personal hygiene [and] carr[y] out personal or household chores." *Ibid.* Yet household chores, bathing, and brushing one's teeth are among the types of manual tasks of central importance to people's daily lives, and should have been part of the assessment of whether respondent was substantially limited in performing manual tasks.

"The District Court noted that at the time respondent sought an accommodation from petitioner, she admitted that she was able to do the manual tasks required by her original two jobs in QCIO. App. to Pet. for Cert. A—36. In addition, according to respondent's deposition testimony, even after her condition worsened, she could still brush her teeth, wash her face, bathe, tend her flower garden, fix breakfast, do laundry, and pick up around the house. App. 32—34. The record also indicates that her medical conditions caused her to avoid sweeping, to quit dancing, to occasionally seek help dressing, and to reduce how often she plays with her children, gardens, and drives long distances. *Id.,* at 32, 38—39. But these changes in her life did not amount to such severe restrictions in the activities that are of central importance to most people's daily lives that they establish a manual-task disability as a matter of law. On this record, it was therefore inappropriate for the Court of Appeals to grant partial summary judgment to respondent on the issue whether she was substantially limited in performing manual tasks, and its decision to do so must be reversed."

[285] Spiegel, Alix, 2012, Struggle For Smarts? How Eastern And Western Cultures Tackle Learning, NPR Morning Edition, November 12, 2012 4:00 AM,

http://www.npr.org/blogs/health/2012/11/12/164793058/struggle...

[286] Naef, Andrea Kloehn, 2012, Toyota Motor Manufacturing v. Williams: A Case of Carpal Tunnel Syndrome Weakens the Grip of the Americans with Disabilities Act, Pepperdine Law Review, Volume 31 | Issue 2 Article 5, p 575, critiquing this Court on three points: a) The Court failed to consider the legislative history of the ADA, b) The "severely restricted" test is a departure from precedent, and c) The suggestion that working is not a major life activity is contrary to precedent;

"As Williams' story illustrates, *Toyota's* unreasonable standard places employees in an impossible situation: many individuals are impaired enough that they are unable to work without some accommodation, but not impaired enough to receive accommodation under the *Toyota* standard.305 This places the burden on the employee to choose either to stop working, or to continue working and risk further injury, which, ironically, may make the employee impaired enough for reasonable accommodation.306 The burden is on the employee even when, as in Williams' case, an employer could easily offer an alternative that would allow the individual to continue to work and be a productive part of society.307 Williams' story is not unique.308 Following *Toyota,* many more similarly situated individuals may become caught in this catch-22 situation and become unable to work.309 This result is clearly incompatible with the ADA's goals of "full participation, independent living, and economic self-sufficiency ' 310 and reduction of "unnecessary expenses resulting from... nonproductivity."311"

CONSTITUTIONAL AND STATUTORY PROVISIONS INVOLVED

First Amendment "Congress shall make no law respecting an establishment of religion, or prohibiting the free exercise thereof; or abridging the freedom of speech, or of the press; or the right of the people peaceably to assemble, and to petition the Government for a redress of grievances."

Second Amendment "the right of the people to keep and bear Arms, shall not be infringed. "

Fourth Amendment "The right of the people to be secure in their persons, houses, papers, and effects, against unreasonable searches and seizures, shall not be violated, and no Warrants shall issue, but upon probable cause, supported by Oath or affirmation, and particularly describing the place to be searched, and the persons or things to be seized."

Fifth Amendment "nor be deprived of life, liberty, or property, without due process of law"

Sixth Amendment "to be informed of the nature and cause of the accusation; to be confronted with the witnesses against him; to have compulsory process for obtaining witnesses in his favor, and to have the Assistance of Counsel for his defense"

Eighth Amendment "nor cruel and unusual punishments inflicted."

Ninth Amendment "The enumeration in the Constitution, of certain rights, shall not be construed to deny or disparage others retained by the people."

Tenth Amendment "The powers not delegated to the United States by the Constitution, nor prohibited by it to the States, are reserved to the States respectively, or to the people."

Fourteenth Amendment "No State shall make or enforce any law which shall abridge the privileges or immunities of citizens of the United States; nor shall any State deprive any person of life, liberty, or property, without due process of law; nor deny to any person within its jurisdiction the equal protection of the laws."

Oklahoma State Code, Title 43A - Mental Health, OSC 43A
Title II of the Americans with Disabilities Act, ADA

Certification

This document is accurate and true to the best of my knowledge and ability. *Certify page*

and word counts here.

Original Signature of Petitioner
Print Name Here   *Sign Name Here*

Certificate of Service

I hereby certify that on or before   *Date here*   I served the same document(s) via (CD-ROM)

X   Regular U.S. Postal Service   Courier Service   In Person Delivery   E-Mail

Name(s) and   To the following:
Address(es):   1.   Clerk of the Court, Supreme Court of the United States, Washington DC 20543

I swear under the penalty of perjury that the foregoing is true and correct.

Executed on   _Date here_____

Sign name here

Original Signature of Petitioner
Print name here
Contact information here

Afterward

On Story Corps on NPR, a mother interviewed her 6th-grade son, asking about the first epileptic seizure he experienced at school. This sweet and intelligent kid spoke about it with the self-possession any Judge could envy. Maybe not the 1905 Judge in Gould who considered seizures "revolting", and (like Oliver Wendell Holmes) consigned such children to be sterilized as worthless to society and unfit to procreate their kind.

What's the difference between the S&M side of medicine and the Tulsa Dungeon Society?

Safe words.

Not unlike the difference between this Court's presumptions and assumptions of the protections of due process, and what actually happens. Whether it believes it or not, recognizes it or not, the Supreme Court of the United States has a moral and ethical responsibility for the un-Constitutional and inhumane results of its Decisions. No Court of good conscience can ignore the innocent people suffering the worst impacts of its decisions, like a child's neglected goldfish, starved and floating belly up in a hot and filthy fish bowl. It must correct its mistakes and vow on its collective soul not to repeat them. Otherwise, it shall be damned by history and its victims as not having one.

Else those of us, abused as children and adults, who wake in the darkest hours of night, with a terrible bleakness tempting and insisting we should end our lives, can never find healing in a world where we are not respected, not allowed to have productive jobs, without decent places to live. Nor shall we have it from a High Court which still hands down that ancient, evil bigotry, calling us unfit to be full and free members of this society.

www.ingramcontent.com/pod-product-compliance
Lightning Source LLC
Chambersburg PA
CBHW080618190526
45169CB00009B/3226